The Animals' Viewpoint
On Dying, Death,
and Euthanasia

Also by Dr. Elizabeth Severino

Books:

Reiki: The Healer's Touch

Do-It-Yourself Vibrant Health: Mind, Body, & Spirit

Diet to Raise Your Spiritual Level

Guide to International Computer Systems Architecture

Audiotapes:

"100 Breaths"

"Extended Energy Breathwork"

The Animals' Viewpoint On Dying, Death, and Euthanasia

Elizabeth Severino, D.D., D.R.S.

THE HEALING CONNECTION
TURNERSVILLE, NJ

The author is donating a portion of the proceeds from this book to benefit animal welfare organizations.

Web-site : http://www.beyond1.com.

First Edition

Designed by Elizabeth Severino

Cover art by Elizabeth Severino

Printed on acid-free recycled paper.

Library of Congress Cataloging-in-Publication Data

The Cataloging-in-Publication Data information is forthcoming.

ISBN 1-888674-99-7

Dedication

To my parents:

My birth father
John J. Girard-diCarlo
October 6, 1910 -
February 2,1962

My birth mother
Elizabeth Patton
(Girard-diCarlo) Ward
January 11, 1924 -
August 6, 2000

My step-father
(My father for 38 years)
William C. Ward
August 16, 1922 -
May 8, 2001

Chief Seattle

Humankind has not woven the web of life. We are but one thread within it. Whatever we do to the web, we do to ourselves. All things are bound together. All things connect.

Acknowledgments

To the thousands of animals
many now crossed over
who have come into my life
as teachers of loving, healing,
dying, death &
euthanasia,
including but not limited to:
Little-Kit
Fluffy
Taffy
Baron Rudoph Henrik Jacob von Knerr,
a.k.a. "Rudy"
(a dachshund, of course!)
Lady Ann Bercomine
Sparkplug
Candy
Grecka
Petronius
Catullus
Galatea
Freda
Pepper
Tara
Max
Bear
Bea
Lucky
Tanaka
Mario
Alex

In Gratitude & Humility,
I Thank you.

Elizabeth

St. John of the Cross

All the creatures ... according to that which each of them has received in itself from God ... each one raises its voice in testimony to that which God is ... each one after its manner exalts God, since it has God in itself.

More Acknowledgments

Tanaka

$\mathcal{I}$extend my gratitude and love to the many care-humans and animal companions who have trusted me to consult with them and who daily help me to learn more. I particularly am grateful to the numerous animal and human companions who through their crossing over, have strengthened my understanding of the nature of death and of life, including the "knowings" that Spirit is One and that the phases in the cycle of life are the same for all of us, whatever costume we're wearing this life-time.

I am deeply appreciative of the humans who have graced my life with support and encouragement, especially when I was experiencing great turmoil and change in my life; and who believed in me even when I wasn't sure I believed in myself. It comes to me to annotate small stories of the specific contributions, as part of my profound thanks.

Dr. Bernie Spector, D.V.M. Bernie, you co-sponsored my first animal communication workshop years ago; brought your daughter and your dog to my second; and brought your veterinary technicians to my third. In our late-night conversations, you have tirelessly answered numerous questions about veterinary health practices, including how examinations are handled, the details of surgical positions, and the way in which veterinarians would most appreciate patient interview information being presented. You willingly collaborated with me to test me at your clinic on the effectiveness of prayer healing through me, for which we now have proven test results. You were the inspiration for the *Euthanasia Prayer*, intended for veterinary health professionals who even though seeing death every day, remain deeply moved every time. I am extraordinarily grateful to you and honored to call you friend.

Eileen Stuckas, Animal Welfare Devotee. Eileen, many years ago, you asked me to do a communication during a healing touch demonstration for PetSmart. You brought to me, a dog that had been mouthing and biting and, deemed unadoptable, was scheduled to be put down. When I communicated with it, in that extremely busy and noisy store environment, the dog immediately understood and stopped the behavior. He requested certain reinforcement, and your commitment to animal well-being is so great, you did what he asked immediately, for twenty minutes, right there, in the aisles of PetSmart! The animal was adopted early the next week. You saw in this event, an extraordinary event, and put the resources of the Voorhees Animal Orphanage behind me to co-sponsor, along with Dr. Bernie Spector, my first animal communication class. Thank you!

Dr. Gabe Reinhardt, D.V.M. Gabe, you first introduced me to naturopathic, homeopathic and Chinese traditional remedies for animals. Having an understanding of the energy of these remedies and interventions, has helped enormously in knowing how to ask the animals questions about their reactions to and viewpoints on the effectiveness of such treatments, and how to send energies to them and sense their responses. Working with you has also helped in knowing when to advise a care-human to immediately seek veterinary attention for an animal. You came to me one day, to ask me for my spiritual support in the sale of your practice to move 300 miles away. I honor your trust in me to align with the Mystery of the Highest Good and support your choice.

Dr. Deva Khalsa, D.V.M., Light Being Extra Ordinaire! Deva, that you are both colleague and friend, is a Gift beyond measure! You've referred to me, many highly unusual cases, which have helped me enormously in fine-tuning my abilities to sense exceptional energies. You've sponsored two workshops on your premises for me to introduce to your clients, what to expect from an animal communicator and how to use one effectively; especially in collaboration with a veterinary health professional. You've allowed me to learn that CATS will delightfully cooperate with me in a seminar designed specifically for them, even if it's many hours long, which I never thought was possible (thank you, CATS!!!)! You've created the opening for your care-humans to come to me so that I can help heal them, too, thereby helping our animal friends even more and creating win-win-win solutions for all concerned. And one of the things I really love about the two of us: we cry at the same things!

Dr. Joan Borysenko, Empowerment Coach. Joan, our journey together to the Bali paradise rests gently and beautifully on my mind and in my heart. Your loving way of empowering women, particularly me, seeing in me, the energy of "healing priestess," is most appreciated. Your humanity, your authenticity, your realization of who you are, and your willingness to give of yourself with humor and insight even when you are physically exhausted, is most humbly appreciated.

Penelope Smith, Animal Communication Specialist. Dear Penelope, your every step graces our planet with Light and Love! You are a role model for me. Your books and tapes influenced me for years before I experienced the delight of meeting you in person. I am so grateful that our time in form consciously overlaps! Your depth of understanding of the currents of our world and your connection to the animals in-fill me with awe. I deeply appreciate your confidence in me. I feel humble in your presence and honor your Light!

Dr. Ron Roth, Spiritual Healer. Ron, you have given me the inestimable gift of being a human teacher and role model of how to have an intimate, conscious, trusting relationship with a loving God. With compassion and humor, you have emphasized your humanity, wrapped around your Divinity. By example you teach the message: "Be who you are!" You have taught me the meaning and way of prayer; you have shown me how to flow Divine healing energy consciously in every moment. I have grown enormously through your workshops and from your work.

Dr. Caroline Myss, Medical Intuitive. Caroline, through you and your work, I have learned to take the spiritual perspective in everything; through you, I am understanding energy anatomy, which I am now applying to animals and the animal-human connection; through you, I have modeled how to be an energy intuitive; and through you, I met your gifted colleague, Dr. Ron Roth. Every time I am in your presence, my consciousness expands. I look forward to the day that I actually understand everything you teach!

Dean and Prayeri Harrison, *Out of Africa Animal Park*, Fountain Hills, Arizona. Dean and Prayeri, your blessed souls operate one of only two Eden experiments on our planet. You gifted me with the extraordinary opportunity to consult on the physical well-being of dozens of formerly wild animals in captivity. Dean, you taught me an invaluable lesson: when presented with a wild animal, *first* ask, "Who are you?" You taught this lesson through a panther whose answer was, "I am an assassin." Lesson learned! Your tigers and then your lions taught me how to scan a much wider range of energy than I had ever scanned before. I then went on to sense many other creatures, including hyenas, a mamba and a Gabon viper, and even helped to hold an energy of administering medication to the snakes. Thank you, Dean and Prayeri, for the gift of your presence, your love, and your commitment to the One.

Rabbi Yosef Serebryanski, Teacher. Yossi, for several years we enthusiastically bartered daily instruction, excited about the unusual energetics of our exchange, respectful of each other's widely different viewpoints and abilities. I taught you energy healing, bio-spirit intuition and animal communication; you taught me Orthodox Judaism, Kabbalah, and Hebrew. Together, we did energy translations of important sections of the Hebrew Wisdom Literature. Frequently, to my surprise, you called me, "spiritually, the most powerful woman in the world." Although I feel far too human to deserve such high commendation, I am grateful to you for your complete conviction about my role in the elevation of human consciousness.

Sathya Sai Baba, East Indian Spiritual Teacher and Healer. Baba, I suspect you have been guiding me far longer than my consciousness realizes. I thought I first "found" you in 1995. Later, I realized that almost every major teacher or author who has influenced me over the past 30 years, is also someone influenced by you, even my Yoga for Americans teacher from the 1970's! I am grateful for your moment-by-moment presence and partnership in my life. I feel awe recalling the time when, perceiving myself beset with unending difficulties and doubting both my connection to the Divine and my life path, I angrily and telepathically demanded big, obvious proofs from you of your direct interest in guiding my life. The following Sunday, an elderly woman from Brooklyn, NY, showed up at my front door. She explained that she had negotiated 3 hours of subways, buses, and taxis to make the trip to me. She handed me a large, full-length color picture of you autographed, "With love, Baba;" two 4-hour videotapes of your teachings; a box of unknown composition full of vibuhti (which always self-fills); and an autographed copy of your *Discourses on the Bhagavad Gita.* Presenting them to me, she smiled simply and said, "These are from Baba." And then there was the day when I again, in frustration, was wondering if you/the Divine really wanted me to do the healing work of light, love, and truth on our planet. I came home to find every horizontal surface in my house completely covered with grey-white dust! I furiously started to vacuum it all up, when "something" made me pause to smell it. I recognized the unique, sweet smell of vibuhti, and realized you had filled my house with it! Perhaps one day, I will be graced with an Inter-View with you. For now, I rejoice in our Inner-View. Namaste!

Elsie Kerns, Reiki Master. Elsie, you attuned me through all levels of Reiki, assisted in focusing my intention on realizing myself as a healer, and introduced me to Barbara Brennan's work. Through you, I first learned about High Self Perception, the auric field, and the reflection of the spiritual, mental and emotional body in the physical body. Through you, I learned impersonalization, the energy of non-compete, and the place of no resistance. Thank you!

Lee Wolf-Widmann, Reiki Master. Lee, for years you have been a consistently loving, supportive and tireless volunteer assistant, first at most of my classes and events, and subsequently with general administrative duties. Your abilities to organize and keep details straight for me is much appreciated, as is your enthusiastic willingness to take on whatever I ask of you! Thank you for your love and support.

Others I wish to thank include Byron Katie Owen, for "The Work," which I have synthesized into "The Experience of Resonance," perhaps the most powerful method available to transcend limiting beliefs and end all suffering from the stories of the mind; Machaelle Small Wright, for the example of her life in behaving as if the God in all life matters; Linda Tellington-Jones, for her T-Touches, which I quickly integrated into my Reiki for animals; empowerment coach Werner Erhardt, for the experience of the idea of the link between actions and words; success coach Anthony Robbins, for the idea of living with passion; life-long friend Charlie Kevlin, for his rigorous compassion in his commitment to my well-being, in spite of my tendencies to work long hours with little sleep and insufficient nutrition; and life-long friend Jim Barr, who first taught by example, how to live a life of no conflict.

–Dr. Elizabeth Severino, Turnersville, NJ

About Tanaka: *Tanaka is an ancient wisdom in the body of an American cocker spaniel. Instead of large spots on his body, he has three giant hearts: one each on the top of his head (crown center); the middle of his back (identity center); and on his hindquarters (center of life and community).*

In 1992, I felt sorely distressed over a relationship issue. As Tanaka walked down the length of my hall, approaching the stairs with the softness of my bed on his mind, I exclaimed in frustration:

"Tanaka! I just don't know who to love!"

Tanaka paused in the hallway, body facing forward. His head turned back over his right shoulder. He contemplated me with measured patience.

"I love whoever God puts in front of me," he replied.

Stunned, I retorted, "But you bark and growl at people sometimes!"

His look changed to that of a Master Teacher beholding a fledgling student.

"I know and honor my boundaries," he observed matter-of-factly. He then threw a humorous glance of invitation at me, turned and continued his walk upstairs.

Charles Darwin

The love for all living creatures is the most noble attribute of man.

Table of Contents

Kinship With All Life

A Simple Decree

I am unified with all creatures I shall ever meet, and they with me, for we are all manifestations of the One Presence.

All God's creatures are my brothers and sisters. I follow the example of the Masters and treat every living thing with kindness.

I recognize the Divine Presence within and around me and in all forms. Divine Presence watches over me and my beloved animal friends and keeps us all safe and healthy.

Gratefully acknowledging and gladly receiving this benediction, I live and move and accept its fullness in love and trust.

If there is anything within me or any other here, that denies this Presence, this Oneness, I release it and let it go now.

And so it is.

Elizabeth

They Shall Teach Thee

But ask now the beasts,
and they shall teach thee;
and the fowls of the air,
and they shall tell thee:
Or speak to the earth,
and it shall teach thee:
and the fishes of the sea
shall declare unto thee.

Job 12:7-8 KJV.

The Topic is Chosen

Sugar

I'm an animal communicator, spiritual healer, and bio-energy therapist. A few years ago, Dana O'Donnell, a magnificent lady extremely active in animal rescue work, asked me to write an article for the rescue publication, *Paws in Thought*. She assured me her readership of 40,000 humans deeply cared about animals and their well-being.

We knew I had many things I could write about. We both speculated a great topic would be animal communicators and how to use animal communicators to help our animals be happier.

I consulted with the animals on this newly assigned writing venture. Happily and expectantly, I asked the animals, *"What topic?"*

I fully anticipated hearing, *"How to Use an Animal Communicator."*

They answered, *"Euthanasia."*

I was stunned. I asked them multiple times. Each time the answer was the same.

I was convinced I wasn't ready to write on what felt to me like a highly controversial and emotional topic. I attempted other articles, including, *"How to Use an Animal Communicator."*

Nothing got written. Whenever my mind turned to euthanasia, I was filled with discomfort and the feeling that I didn't understand enough to write about it.

Enter our animal friends! The animals have always been incredibly powerful, wonderful, and self-less sources of love and lessons for me. Dana had asked me to write for her; the animals had chosen the topic. The original article was written, yet the lessons have continued. The little book you hold in your hands now, is an outgrowth of the original article. The animals have requested that I make this additional information and perspective available to all.

It is my profound hope that readers will find the lessons and experiences that I write about in these pages, as illuminating as I have in writing about them. This book is not intended to be any kind of final word on the nature of the cycles of life and the dimensions in between. It is, however, a recounting of my direct experiences over the course of many decades. Very simply, I know how much it hurts to lose an animal (or any!) companion we love. What I hope to accomplish more than anything, is to gift my translation of the clarity and perspective of the animals' viewpoints on dying, death, and euthanasia, to loving care-humans wanting to make conscious decisions involving the lives of the animal companions entrusted to them, thereby minimizing grief and dispelling doubt. Bessie Stanley in 1905 said: *"To know that even one life has breathed easier because you have lived, this is to have succeeded."*

About Sugar: Sugar is an Arabian Mare/Morgan in British Columbia who is in a profound co-healing partnership with her human. Sugar was reflexing her loving care-human, Adrien, by experiencing laminitis and assorted infections. At one point, her human had ceased riding her and there was great concern for Sugar. Reiki and Prayer energy were invoked for both on a regular basis.

Her human awakened even more to her spirituality, began to see and face the Truth of her life, and even eventually realized that she, too (the human), was experiencing health problems caused by issues with her feet! As Adrien healed, she asked if Sugar might be happier with a move to a new stable. Sugar said, "Yes," and was moved to a new stable. At 27 years of age, Sugar has returned to health, wholeness and vitality, and both now enjoy riding together again.

Part I:

On Dying and Death

Mohandas Gandhi

The greatness of a nation and its moral progress can be judged by the way its animals are treated.

Norma

Semantic, Legal, Moral, Ethical, Religious, Spiritual & Emotional Issues

Euthanasia.

The very word evokes an emotional response in most people. The meaning . . . the morality . . . the ethics . . . the legality . . . the religious implications . . . the spirituality . . . the questions . . . the decision . . . the aftermath.

Euthanasia. In Greek, which as a Dean's List student at Vassar College I studied for years, it means a painless, happy death. *Eu* means well, or good. *Thanatos* means death. A good death.

Thucydides, Homer, Plutarch, Plato and other Greek poets and writers called death, *thanatos*, "the twin brother to sleep." The Greeks and later the Romans did not consider life as needing to be preserved at all cost and were quite tolerant of suicide or assisted death in situations of necessity when no other relief could be offered to the dying, or in the case of the Stoics or Epicureans, where a person of humanistic leaning no longer cared for his life. Euthanasia then meant an easy and painless death; a painless method of dying.

Euthanasia did not always infer involvement in the death process of a party other than the one dying. Up until the 20th Century, it simply meant to die well. English Physician John Arbuthnot (1675-1735) once said:

"The kindest wish of my friends is euthanasia."

In the English language, in the past hundred or so years, we have come to use the root word euthanasia as a verb, *to euthanize*, to mean the painless causing of death, by one other than the dying. Usually the intent is to end suffering. The end to suffering is most certainly what one would hope, whenever we make the choice to euthanize a beloved animal friend who is suffering and/or incurably ill.

Accepted and even expected in certain circumstances in certain cultures, in Western culture, euthanasia is controversial. Performed on humans in the United States, for example, it is exceptionally controversial and legal only in the form, assisted suicide, in the state of Oregon. Performed on humans, elsewhere in the world, it is legal in the forms euthanasia and assisted suicide only in the Netherlands.

The difference between euthanasia and assisted suicide is who performs the act after which death occurs. With euthanasia, legally, it is now defined as someone other than the one dying. With assisted suicide, it is the one dying.

It seems the height of this controversy in our time stems from events beginning in the fall of 1939 in Nazi Germany, where "mercy killings" were performed on children three and under who were deemed imperfect, unviable, or incapable of life worth living. This later expanded to old, ill, or infirm adults; and from there turned into attempted genocide.

Among health professionals, euthanasia and/or assisted death for humans has been dissuaded for millennia. Hippocrates, the "Father of Modern Medicine," stated in his Hippocratic Oath around 400 BC, "I will give no deadly medicine to any if asked, nor suggest any such counsel."

This may have been his advice, but I can affirm, as a former Vassar College Dean's List Classics student, that then as now, obtaining deadly medicine was pretty easy for anyone who wanted it and suicide was not uncommon.

Dr. Jack Kevorkian's work in North America has been

thought-provoking and controversial. It catapulted the debate around euthanasia and assisted suicide into a situation of high-profile public policy and the law.

Legal issues involving animals include animals as property and owner's rights to the disposition of that property. Laws protect animals and ensure their humane treatment. The Humane Society of the United States decrees, "All animals that need to be killed, whether it is for food, for humane reasons, or because they are homeless, must receive a quick and painless death." Laws also require the elimination of animals under certain circumstances and conditions. There are rules and procedures for such elimination as humanely as possible.

Among religious communities, depending on the religion, the issues relative to animals deal with a wide range of questions. Some religions question whether animals have souls and are worthy of consideration. Some religions state that man has dominion over all the animals; their interpretation of "dominion" subsumes allowing man to do whatever he wants with all creatures. Some religions teach that euthanasia is another word for murder. Others religions teach that all life is to be honored and respected.

Spiritual issues recognize the oneness, the kinship of all life. This subsumes the innate need of the soul, regardless of its form, for gentle honoring; and the continual oneness of the cycle of life, with emphasis on grace and dignity in all phases of life.

Ethical and moral issues concern right human conduct. The assumption here is that human consciousness is capable of acting from principle superseding instinct. We have the potential, this position affirms, to be concerned not only with our own welfare but also with the welfare of human society, all creatures on the planet, indeed the life of the planet as a whole. Positions here range from the teachings of the world-view of negation, as taught by Indian thinkers and ancient Christianity; to affirmation of the world, as taught by the prophets of Israel, the sages of China, and European thinkers of the Renaissance era; to the current day search for the balance necessary in recognizing that we are living as spirits having a human experience.

The questions agonizing humans frequently ask themselves in their times of profound love and pain, anticipating the extraordinary grief of separation from a beloved companion while witnessing its aging or suffering, include, *"Is euthanasia really right at all? Is it just another word for murder? Should I 'do' it? Do I have the right? When should I do it? What is the most humane and loving thing to do now?"*

And the most important question for most care-humans, in their love and their pain, is, *"How will I know if this is right?"*

The aftermath of a decision to euthanize, in addition to the deep sense of loss and grief, often also includes guilt, especially if some of the factors the human entered into the equation of the decision included knowledge of expensive yet iffy interventions declined; the inconvenience of caring for the very ill; and pressure from well-meaning friends.

And then there's doubt.

Performed on companion animals, euthanasia is always highly personal for the humans making the decision(s). Often, the humans making such decisions for their companion animals experience exceptional pain, emotional suffering and grief. Most remember the animal, the decision, and the event for the rest of their lives.

Natural ethics, I have observed, is entirely subjective, transcending in the moment all structure of philosophy, morality, law, or religion. It is a truth that the human species faces ongoingly the decisions between killing and letting live in situations other than dire necessity. In the phenomenal world, we view continually the spectacle of one life preserving itself by fighting and/or killing another. Yet in the human world, we acknowledge that a higher spirit of omnipresent loving-kindness is possible.

Albert Schweitzer once observed, "In the universe, the will to live is in conflict with itself. In us, it seeks to be at peace with itself... Reverence for life, arising when intelligence operates upon the will to live, contains within itself affirmation of the universe and of life."

I currently believe that reverence for life is the only workable principle, subsuming as it does both love and compassion for all creatures everywhere. I have noticed that if all life is not regarded as intrinsically valuable, human relations to self, God, nature, and our fellow humans, disintegrate. To quote Albert Schweitzer again: "By ethical conduct toward all creatures, we enter into a spiritual relationship with the universe."

A basis for reverence for all life is the taking of life only from necessity. This infers total conscious action, the understanding of the true role of the human species as care-takers with loving dominion over the planet, and finding and living the balance between physical life at all costs and physical death.

But this is all from the human perspective.

About Norma: *Norma's care-human Jennifer used to hold her against her heart for hours, as shown in this picture, becoming very adept at "going about my chores one-handed." Norma was an extremely highly elevated, gracious and very courageous hedgie whose experience of life and death deeply touched every soul.*

Sir Wilfred Grenfell

Kindness to all God's creatures is an absolute rock-bottom necessity if peace and righteousness are to prevail.

Death Experience

Rudy and Me - 1956

*I*mmediately after the animals chose the topic of euthanasia and I finally accepted the assignment, they began to involve me in new experiences of living, healing, dying, death, and euthanasia. It became increasingly clear the animals had a very important and urgent message they wanted me to understand and then to share. A new phase, at some points a very painful phase of remembrance, growth and learning in my life began.

Memories of extremely painful past experiences long buried reappeared, clearly being raised to surface consciousness by the urgent need of the animals for me to understand and communicate their point of view. I can see now, that the recall of these memories, indeed the very experiencing of them and the ability to comprehend them from my current perspective, was critical in my ability to understand what the animals were now telling me.

In each of the memories, was a lesson.

New experiences also presented, again, many painful ones. Links were created to previous experiences, with a new way of looking at them, through which I could now grasp a larger message.

I have found that as I have taught the animals' viewpoints in my animal communication classes and explained the formative events that were brought again to memory as the animals were teaching me, that my students have asked repeatedly that I write them up. My students have told me that both the recounting of the stories and equally importantly the learnings I have shared, that have come from those lessons, have been very helpful to them. In that spirit, I now relate some of the formative experiences which have helped me understand

and relate to the animals' viewpoints.

♡   ♡   ♡

As is true for many of us, my life has been powerfully impacted by death. For me, it started very young. My earliest remembrances of a death experience occurred as a 4-1/2-year-old child. My family then lived on a large farm in beautiful Chester Springs, PA. One of our feral cats had given birth. Unbeknownst to us at the time, she had hidden her kittens below the floor-boards of the large wooden-planked porch flanking the side of the old farm house. The feral cat herself then disappeared.

My Mother noticed this and enrolled me in finding the newborn kittens, knowing their lives were endangered, at risk from predators and starvation. We scoured our property.

We first heard the kitten sounds coming from under the porch planking. Mother fetched a crow-bar from the tool shed and pried up the floor-boards about a foot and a half away from the area seeming to be the source of the mewing. She then lowered her slender, athletic body, flashlight in hand, into the dark, wet hollow below the porch boards.

Carefully, one at a time, she handed the kittens up to me. I placed them in a basket Mother had already lined with towels and hot water bottles. The two of us began, one kitten at a time, to feed the newborns warm milk from small droppers. They fed hungrily.

One of the kittens couldn't walk. When propped up, it fell over instantly. It seemed to have little muscle control anywhere in its body. None of its functions appeared correct. Its tongue lolled out of its mouth. Its eyeballs rolled.

"It has polio," my Mom announced. "Don't feed it."

Looking back, I comprehend the influence of that disease on my parents' generation.

"Don't feed it?" I started to register what she was saying.

"Why?" I remember asking.

"It's not going to live," Mother replied simply.

I looked at the kitten. I felt it saying "Yes" to me, acknowledging my Mom was correct. I watched the little kitten, fascinated at its inability to move. I felt wonder at the idea of the little kitten dying. I felt wonder at how peaceful the kitten seemed, even though it could hardly move. I named the kitten, "Little-Kit," and put her in my lap, comforting her and talking to her, while dropper-feeding the other kittens. Shortly, my Mother lifted her from me.

Little-Kit seemed comfortable in my Mother's knowledgeable and compassionate hands. There was great love, great appreciation. Mother loved animals. Mother stroked and petted the kitten, talking to it. Mother seemed to be explaining something to the kitten. I didn't hear all of what she said, but I knew great loving and tenderness were being shared. In what I did hear, she spoke to the kitten about her view of Heaven and being directly with God, and about what the kitten could expect next. I remember wondering about where Heaven was, and why it might be better to be there than here. I remember feeling that the expression of love and tenderness felt correct and balanced.

I learned that it is correct and appropriate under certain circumstances, to gently, compassionately and quickly assist animals who cannot otherwise survive, in crossing over. I learned that animals can know when they are going to die. I learned that I really care about animal well-being and the relationship between animals and humans; and that loving relationships felt correct.

I was extremely fortunate during our years on the farm in the early 1950's that my uncle, Robert Patton, was an animal communicator and hands-on healer. Whenever he visited, we would spend time together, walking in the woods, or talking to anything and everything .... animals, plants, insects, the trees, the pond, the clouds.

It never occurred to me that everyone didn't do this and because he was available to me to talk to about it and share, I never much talked to anyone else about it, except occasionally my Mom, who never responded. My uncle subsequently moved to Loveland, CO, where he shared his gift with considerable local renown until his death.

As soon as I could read, I started reading books about animals. According to my elementary school report cards from the Baldwin School, in Bryn Mawr, PA, in the second grade alone I had read 60 books and had already reached the vocabulary and comprehension of a fifth grader. This was deemed "a noteworthy achievement since she is a full year younger than the other children in her grade." The report card continues to observe that almost all of the books were about animals. There was a caution to the next year's teacher, to try to encourage me to expand my interests.

I continued to want to read about animals and their relationships with people; and only somewhat less frequently, about plants and people. I "got away" with this for almost three more years.

One event burns in my memory from that second-grade year. One of our dogs died. I was crying and distraught when my Dad drove me to school that morning. I was late for Mrs. Meyer's class. As was required, we went to the head mistress, my Dad and I. My Dad explained the situation, and I was "released" to go to class.

I opened the door to the classroom. Mrs. Meyers sternly said, "You're late."

I replied, "My dog died this morning." I started to cry again.

"Go to your seat. You have seat work to do and you're late."

I felt devastated by the harshness and apparent total lack of understanding and complete absence of sympathy. I cried as I went to my seat and took out my workbook. My tears blinded me and I couldn't see the pages. I felt the reaction from some of the other students, compassionate, yet not daring to speak.

I created the belief that not everyone understands or knows how to react to the depth of feeling that accompanies the loss of a beloved animal companion.

♡   ♡   ♡

I continued my passion for animals and anything and everything about them. In my fifth grade year, however, there was a major confrontation. I still wanted to read about animals, learn about animals, draw animals, sculpt animals, model animals, experience everything I could about animals.

My fifth-grade teacher, Mrs. James, kept telling me to expand my range of interests. The "straw" for her, was when we got to the poetry module; we were to choose and memorize a poem. Except she refused to let me choose my own poem. She assigned me, *"The Village Blacksmith,"* very proud of herself that it had nothing to do with animals and even announcing this to my class. I was very embarrassed at being singled out in this way. I felt totally humiliated. And then I got angry. And after that, I caught an idea that so inspired me I launched full-steam into implementing it!

Instead of reciting *"The Village Blacksmith"* as originally written, with my already-acknowledged and extraordinary command of English, I re-wrote it as *"The Village Squirrel."* I did not, however, tell anyone of my actions.

When it was my turn, Mrs. James called me to the head of the room during assembly for my recitation. As I announced *"The Village Squirrel, with apologies to Henry Wadsworth Longfellow,"* I glanced laterally at her and saw her eyes bulge with dis-belief. I heard joyful laughter from my fellow students and since I by then had friends in all the grades, the reaction was pretty substantial. Widened eyes and broad smiles of anticipation adorned the faces of the teachers present, most of whom had long ago decided I was delightfully creative and anticipated anything I did.

I began my recitation:

Within the spreading chestnut tree, the village squirrel sits;

The squirrel, a wondrous creature he, with quick and crafty wits;
And the muscles of his practiced jaw spit out his acorn pits.

His hair is rough, brown-red, and short;
His face is towards the sun; ...

I continued until the very end of my (I thought) brilliant parody.

My fellow school mates were totally delighted. There was much laughter and lively appreciation. As I thought they might, other teachers nodded in joyful alignment with the creativity, humor and perfect meter and rhyme of the re-written poem.

Mrs. James, however, was furious. She enrolled the school's head mistress in her position. Both my parents were called in for a conference. It was decided that I would be forbidden to read about, do reports on or engage in any projects involving animals.

I was beside myself, devastated and heart-broken beyond description. I cried for weeks. I didn't want to do any work at all. School, which up until then I had loved, became horrible to me. I started to hate my teacher, in my youth forgetting that I was the one who not only had "broken the rules" but had openly defied the authority of my teacher. I created the belief that there are rules, major rules, that adults care deeply about, and that following or breaking rules has equally major consequences.

My misery continued until one day, I realized that I was taking the Paoli Local train from the Haverford station to the Bryn Mawr station, completely by myself. I further realized that only our house-man was home when I got home; that the Bryn Mawr train station, which is where I got off to walk to Baldwin, was very close to the public library in Bryn Mawr; and that I could easily spend time in the library after school and take a later train home! No one except the librarian and our house-man, who adored me and would never tell my parents, would know!

Guided by the planet's most wonderful librarian and protected by the world's most supportive house-man, I discovered a whole new world of adventure, freedom and learning in the library. I explained to the librarian that I couldn't take the books home. She gave me a cubicle of my own, where I could leave whatever books I wanted. She never once asked me to officially check them out with a library card.

I learned how incredibly wonderful experiencing life and learning from books could be! I felt totally supported by two loving people aligned with my heart's desires. I learned that when the heart is set with intention towards learning and love, the Universe moves in response and will employ others, even total strangers, to help express its goodness.

A few years later, when I was an eight-year old child, my family had a loveable mutt named Fluffy. By then we were living on College Avenue in Haverford, PA. Fluffy and I played and romped together on the beautiful grounds of Haverford College, across the street from our house. We frequently crossed the quiet road together to reach the college campus.

On another day burned into my memory, Fluffy suddenly and completely uncharacteristically bolted across our lawn way ahead of me. He went full speed into the road and collided with a garbage truck which ran completely over him.

I streaked across the long lawn screaming to Fluffy, to the men on the truck, to anyone, for help. One of the men quickly picked up Fluffy's body and threw it on top of the open garbage heap. Looking me straight in the eye, he wordlessly mounted the step on the back of the truck, twice hitting the side of the truck, apparently signaling the driver. The truck then sped away.

I ran after it, down the middle of the road. I screamed to the truck to stop.

It didn't.

The truck quickly out-distanced me.

I returned home, running into the house, gasping my story out to my Mother. There was great confusion. Mother called local township officials and did her best to find and retrieve Fluffy's body. We never heard from them or saw him again. It felt wrong, horribly wrong.

I learned how quickly a loved animal companion can be gone. I learned how quickly life can change. I learned that animals either sometimes **don't** appear to know that they are going to die; or that they act according to an invisible plan. I learned that animals sometimes don't understand moving vehicles, or how to avoid them. I learned the horrible feeling of powerlessness over events. I learned that I cared about what happened to the bodies of the animals I loved. I re-learned that I wanted to be with them and comfort them when they were hurt.

Our College Avenue house burned down soon after this incident and we moved into another house in Haverford, this one on Craig Lane. There again were many animals, long lawns, beautiful grounds. Again we had dogs, this time a German Shepherd named Grecka and a dachshund named Baron Rudolph Henrik Jacob Von-Knerr, a.k.a. Rudy. My Dad had a great sense of humor and he felt a long dog needed a long name!

At the age of 12, I was accepted into Ron Ziegler's "Dog Obedience Training" classes with our German Shepherd. Ron took a special liking to me and spent a great deal of time with me. Grecka and I actually entered obedience trials through Ron and we did very well.

I am eternally grateful for having had this wonderful very early experience with canine-human cooperation education. During this time I learned that the result had much more to do with training the human than training the animal friend, since Grecka always seemed to know what was going on. I was clear I was the one that needed "training."

♡   ♡   ♡

At the Craig Lane house, a bird and I became friends. It always looked for me when I was outside and I for it. When I would ride my bike or take long walks, the bird would often accompany me, no matter how long the ride or how spontaneous the trail for the walks. We always seemed to know where the other was.

One afternoon I felt drawn to the bushes separating our home from our neighbors. I found my friend lifeless.

Carefully I picked him up. I didn't cry. I did feel an unusual energy completely envelop me. I remember thinking, *"What happened?"* and seeing in my mind, a picture of the bird flying and being hit by something and falling.

I told the bird how much I had loved talking to it, how much I loved that it would sing to me whenever it saw me and accompany me whenever I took my walks or rode my bike.

I went into our house and found my younger brother and a shoe box. Then we visited the garage and found a small shovel and some clean rags from our rag bag. We lined the shoe box with the rags and took the shoe-box coffin and the shovel outside. Gently I placed my friend's little body into the box.

Slowly, with long, deliberate strides, carrying the box with the body of my precious little friend, we moved across our yard to a soft place of ground beyond our trees. I placed the shoe box on the ground. My brother dug a shallow grave.

We put the shoe box next to the grave and spent some time with the bird. I talked to it. I sang to it. I spoke child-mind words of flying wherever it wanted, of freedom and endless sky. After a while, we placed the shoe box in the ground and covered it with dirt. My eyes teared, but only for a few minutes and only when I felt the "no more" of shared times. It all felt right, correct, appropriate.

I learned I liked honoring my animal friends in the phases of their lives. It felt whole and complete and correct.

A few weeks later, my brother wondered what had happened to the bird's body. Awareness of my friend came into my consciousness and stayed with me while we dug up the little grave. We saw the body. It was decomposing and had none of the energy of my friend about it. We buried it again. I learned there is a clear distinction between the physical body and the essence energy after physical death.

Two years later we moved again, this time to an apartment on Montgomery Avenue in Haverford. I wanted an allowance and my parents told me that I would have to work for any money. There were many dogs in the apartment building so I started a dog-walking business. The charge was $.25 per dog per walk, so a two-dog walk was $.50. Three, two-dog walks a day was the amazing amount of $1.50! I had customers in the apartment building and I was thrilled! I loved walking, playing with and feeding the dogs and visiting, playing with and feeding the cats. I made enough money so that my Dad, in my first experience of a "matching-grant" program, matched my funds and together we bought me my very first dog of my own, a black and white Cocker Spaniel I named Sparkplug.

I loved Sparkplug more than any other dog I'd ever had. I groomed him, "trained" him, fed him, walked him. He slept on my bed. We were inseparable.

One day, Sparkplug and I went visiting, to the Ardmore house of one of my girl-friends, Zoe Kelly. We were sitting in her living room, playing, when her father came home. He smiled faintly at us and said he didn't feel well. He looked very colorless. He asked Zoe to tell her Mom that he was going upstairs to take a nap.

Zoe and I watched him as he started to ascend the open stairs from the first floor to the second. His hand went to his chest and he let out a desperate rattle-groan sound then fell backwards, hitting his head on the stairs as his body half slid and half bounced towards the open landing.

Zoe screamed and ran into the kitchen to get her mother. Sparkplug started to bark. I held onto Sparkplug and watched, horrified, as Zoe's dad crumpled in a heap on the landing.

Zoe and her mom came running in from the kitchen. As she ran up the stairs, she saw me and yelled, "Go home!"

I didn't know what else to do so I went home. I didn't say anything about the situation to anyone. Hours later, Zoe's mom called to speak with my Mom and asked how I was doing. She then explained to my surprised mother, what had happened, saying that her husband had suffered a heart attack and had fallen backwards down the stairs and died right in front of me.

I was clutching Sparkplug in my bedroom, wondering again at how quickly life ends, how quickly life changes. But I both noticed and paid attention to the complete lack of color around Zoe's dad's body when he came into the house and climbed the stairs right before he died and while he was dying. I had seen that before. I was to see it many times again.

When Sparkplug was about two years old we moved to Rosemont, PA. Our home was again on a busy road, Montgomery Avenue, but still with the large grounds my parents so loved.

I was very involved in after-school activities. One day I came home, sensing that something was very wrong. I had taken the late bus and that meant dinner was served as soon as I arrived, since I was the last one home. We all sat at the table. I looked for our dogs, especially Sparkplug, but they weren't in the house. I knew that sometimes Mom left them outside, yet still there was something very wrong.

As we all sat down at the table, my Dad turned to me and said, "Sparkplug was killed today. He was run over."

I choked. I cried. I felt a huge wave of compassion come from both my brothers, who clearly already knew and equally clearly had been told to be quiet. Dinner time in our house was usually not a time of happiness and light. It was a time used to mold and teach us, particularly my older brother, and we did not speak unless spoken to.

My Mom barked out, "Don't cry at the dinner table. Eat your dinner."

I couldn't eat. I couldn't do anything. I wanted to run to my room but I knew I would be severely punished for that, since leaving the dinner table before one was excused was a serious crime in our house.

"We'll get you another dog right away," my Dad said.

"Another dog?" I remember thinking. I didn't want another dog, I wanted Sparky. My buddy was gone. I had worked for a year to earn my half of the money needed to buy him, had trained him, fed him, cared for him, played with him, loved him, enjoyed him, let him sleep in my bed. There could be no replacement for him.

I loved my Dad and looked deeper at his feelings. I realized again, this time from a place of understanding, that a human who has never had his own animal companion, as my Dad never had, does not usually understand the depth of attachment and the sense of great loss, that someone who unconditionally loves an animal companion and loses it, can feel.

My Dad did what he said. A few days later he came home with another cocker spaniel, which came from the Francisville animal orphanage near us. Taffy was named for her color. She absorbed my grief and accepted my love.

Taffy sensed my profound pain over the loss of Sparky

immediately. She quickly became attached to me, following me around, always there for me. She had a wonderful habit of softly licking my face and the backs of my hands, which I found very comforting.

I learned again how sensitive animal friends can be to our emotions; how soothing and healing the unconditional love of an animal friend can be.

A few weeks after Taffy joined our house, when I was just beginning to mend, with her help, from missing Sparkplug, I returned home triumphant! My high school lacrosse team, on which I played center, had just won the championships and I had scored the goal that had given us the lead! I was excited, thrilled! Still wearing my white Harriton Varsity uniform, riding home on the late bus, I flew down the school bus steps in front of my house!

Taffy was across the street in a neighbor's yard. She saw me and abandoning her normal behavior of being car-aware, she immediately ran into the street. Just as quickly, a passing station wagon ran over her.

Horrified and screaming, I raced for Taffy. The driver stopped immediately. Taffy wasn't moving. Her eyes were glazed over. Her tongue was lolling out of her mouth, from which blood was seeping.

I picked Taffy up. Her blood gushed all over my white uniform. The lady had a small piece of plywood in her vehicle. We put Taffy on the plywood. We raced to a veterinarian's office, whose location the lady knew, driving into the back parking lot.

I waited with Taffy while the lady ran into the office. Almost immediately, the veterinarian and the lady emerged from the back office door.

The veterinarian looked at Taffy.

"This dog is dead," he said.

Moving very quickly, he picked up Taffy's body by the collar and threw her into the trash dumpster in the back of his building. Still moving very quickly, he went into his building, closed and audibly locked the back door.

I was stunned and so was the lady, who approached the back door and pounded on it. She then seemed to realize something. Looking at me in an unusual way, she suddenly said, "I need to take you home. Now. Get back in the car."

"What about Taffy?" I demanded.

"I'm sorry. I'm really sorry. But there's nothing we can do. I have to take you home. Now."

The thought flashed through my mind that she was worried about the fact that we had simply jumped into the car and left my house and that she was now here with me and my dead dog without my parents' knowledge. I felt in my heart that leaving at that time was wrong but I also felt her great and sudden concern.

The whole thing was wrong. The body shouldn't have been left there, certainly not in a trash dumpster. I wanted Taffy's body back, at least to bury her. But I did as the increasingly distraught woman demanded.

I was strengthening the internal knowing that bodies need to be honored.

Shortly after this wretched experience, my two paternal uncles and my paternal grandfather died. At my grandfather's funeral, my father cried. This was the first time in my life I had ever seen my Dad cry. His heart was so broken. His body started to lose color. I had a fear of what that meant. I had seen that before. I wrote about this in my high school English creative composition class, receiving an A+ with the comment, "Shows intuition and wisdom way beyond your tender years."

It was not a happy A+. It was a time I clearly did NOT want to be right.

A month after my composition, my birth father died suddenly, late at night, of a heart attack.

In the midst of the confusion, the police, the ambulance, the Doctor roused suddenly from sleep and with liquor on his breath, the subsequent screams and cries of despair from my Mom; my Mom and my older brother with my Dad and the ambulance team in my parents' bedroom, I sat huddled in the door-jamb of my room, right across from my parents' bedroom and in clear view, watching. Quiet, unnoticed, afterwards, when my Mother and older brother were downstairs with officials, I again watched while two undertakers entered my parents' bedroom.

I observed the two men struggling with my Dad's body.

"He's really heavy," one man said.

My youth-mind could not fathom how anyone could think someone I loved as much as my Dad could be heavy. When they finally got his body into the body bag and started to zip it up, my Dad's left arm suddenly flipped out of the black bag. The two men swore mightily, unzipped the bag and attempted to stuff my Dad's arm back in it. They succeeded, swearing the whole time, finally zipping up the bag and carrying my Dad's body away.

The bodies of those who have died needed to be honored, I had already decided. I now decided that the honoring needed to include the attitude and the words of virtually all the people around them.

Two months after my Dad died, my best friend's beloved grandmother died. I was still very fresh from the wound of the loss of my Dad, however, Kathy Cook, my dear friend, was distraught. I took the train and then walked to the funeral parlor to be with her for the viewing. She was so grateful to see me that she ran up to me and threw her arms around me. My very presence was a great comfort to her.

Kathy and I had been friends for many years. I knew her family and she knew mine. I noticed some particularly loud people crying and looking distraught, dressed in black, over near her grandmother's coffin. I didn't recognize any of them. I asked Kathy who they were.

"They're professional mourners," Kathy said. "My Mom and Dad hired them, to make it look like my Grandmother knew more people than she did. But what's happening is, my Mom feels better because she can see someone crying along with her."

I learned that shared grief is grief starting to heal.

Within a few months after this event, a school girl friend was killed in an automobile accident and all of my beloved animals either were killed or had been given away. It was a period of extreme emotional pain, grief, and subsequent extensive turmoil. I learned to fear the finality and emptiness of the death process and its aftermath, especially the depth of emotions released and the changes unpredicted. I learned to doubt religion and thinking God was religion, learned to doubt God, wondering how could a God of love cause such pain in anyone's life?

I became an agnostic and wrote a poem, *"The Steeple,"* first published when I was 16 years of age:

"The Steeple"

My philosophy of life?
Do I think that in men, strife
Would dominate if all
Were left only to nature's call?

Or do I think that men would be
Ruled by love and charity?
E'en then, how would I act,
If aught of this, were proved as fact?

Ah, I now can see myself,
Searching through some dusty shelf,
Trying hard to see,
What beliefs would just suit ME.

But I am not of such a mind.
It seems too hard to try to find
A basis for my steeple.
And so I'll stop, and join the people.

In spite of this poem or perhaps because of it, I began a life-long search for Truth. The search for the Truth in living subsumes the search for the Truth in dying; both inextricably lead to the Truth of the dimensions in between. The search for Truth thus encompasses explorations of the evolution of consciousness and this leads to embracing Mystery. Understanding and accepting Mystery and the Awe of living, leads naturally to understanding and accepting the Mystery and Awe of dying. Any involvement with Mystery teaches that Mystery lies beyond belief, beyond words.

We all inherit the human condition of mind and mind's ruthless compassion in showing us every place we think we're separate or disconnected from the experience of Experience. As we progress in consciousness, we realize that we are not our minds, yet we have minds; and that minds have thoughts, beliefs, feelings and opinions, all borrowed from the Master database of consciousness. As we understand Mind more and understand the One-ness that lives beyond Mind more, we find true ecstacy in Existence.

But I didn't know that, then.

It's taken me most of my life to discover that all systems of thought, all belief systems, are guides only, and that Absolute Truth lies beyond beliefs, theories, or ideologies; and that its joyful Being is available to all of us.

But in my then youthful quest, I started with established beliefs, including religion and philosophy, in which I have been passionately interested my entire life. I also began to take self-empowerment and consciousness-raising workshops. I eventually even earned a Doctorate in Religious Studies.

One early self-empowerment workshop I experienced was the Werner Erhardt "6-Day," an intensive, rigorous personal growth and development program. During my "6-Day," we did a process called, "The Samurai Game." I was chosen as a warrior for the Samurai Game. There were many, many rules to this Game, some of them quite strange to me.

The rules included recognizing the leader of our team as a God to be immediately and instantly obeyed. Because he was a God, the rules said, we were not allowed to look upon his face. Doing so would be interpreted as treason and the perpetrator would be executed immediately.

I, however, was trained well by my Mother to look at someone when s/he was addressing me. At a particularly vigorous portion of our Leader's exhortations and pre-battle pep-talk, our Leader directly addressed me. I reflexively raised my bowed head to look at him.

The command came instantly.

"Die!" my Leader shouted.

I was "executed" on the spot.

"So quick," I thought. *"I didn't mean it."* But I had definitely broken the rules. Again.

For a few minutes, I lay where I had "fallen." I acknowledged my error. I contemplated my empowerment and honoring of authorities over the years of my life, plus the dis-empowerment and dis-honoring of authorities. I contemplated the rules of authorities, plus my rules of behavior learned in childhood and different rules from different cultures, including the several countries I had by then visited.

I remembered the "rules" as they had been explained to us for what to do when we had been "killed." We were to lie wherever and precisely how we had fallen and keep our eyes totally closed. If a "body-tender" approached us we were to cooperate, keeping our eyes closed while remembering that we were dead.

Warriors were not body-tenders. Each group was coached with different rules and did not know the other's rules. I did not know what the body-tenders had been told.

Body-tenders approached me shortly. They straightened out the limbs of my body, stroked my head and hair. They spoke to me of bravery and willingness to fight for our cause.

"Bravery?" I remember wondering. *"I never even engaged in battle! I was executed for treason!"*

No matter, to the body-tenders. The fact that I had shown up, was enough. I was being honored with the utmost gentleness and respect for being a warrior and for my time in form as a human being.

I was taken off the "battlefield" and placed in a room where, eyes closed, I sensed many other "dead" bodies had been lain.

My consciousness, of course, was still quite intact.

Again I was honored. My body was ceremonially "cleaned," hair brushed, face washed. Soothing sounds were spoken. My face was eventually completely covered with a very light cloth.

Although part of me wondered why there was so much of a big deal being made about a now useless dead person-body ... *"I'm dead, what's the point?"* ... deep down I knew that the honoring, the ritual, the soothing words, the gentleness, was speaking to my consciousness, my spiritual awareness, and was correct. It felt superb. I was keenly and exceptionally aware of it.

I remained there until the end of the "game," at which point I came to life again and returned to the seminar.

I "experienced" death as a death of the physical body only. I was beginning to understand the experience of the continuity of consciousness. This would be confirmed years later, when I had an actual near-death experience.

The intervening decades have given me many, many additional experiences with death and dying. I've assisted in or been involved in the passing of many dozens of humans and hundreds of animals.

By 1994, I had become a professional healer, using modalities including Reiki, Prana, Huna, and QiGong. I was also a competitive ballroom dancer, a passionate hobby. I had a very dear friend, "Chuck," who was one of the most delightful dancers in my geographical area. Always positive and full of joy, he knew and let you know, that for him the dance experience was an opportunity to connect on the dance floor in a beautiful way.

After Chuck's forced retirement he received what for him became the opportunity of his life: a dance chaperon on cruise ships. He danced the great ocean liners of the world, taking the most wonderful, round-the-world cruises to exotic places! Whenever he was in the area, which was infrequently, he would glow and delight gratefully in how wonderful his life was!

I saw him in July, 1994, and was surprised to find him ill. He had come to watch me perform at a dance exhibition. He explained he would stay to watch me dance and then would leave. He had caught pneumonia, he said, on a cruise to the British Isles and didn't know it until weeks later. He was confident he would soon recover.

I was very surprised one October morning to receive a call from a dear mutual friend advising me that she had just found out that Chuck was in the University of Pennsylvania Hospital in Philadelphia and he was not expected to live.

"What happened?" I asked. "Exactly where is he?"

I immediately made arrangements to go to him. In his hospital room I found his son, who had flown in from California, and his daughter, from Southern New Jersey. Both were praying fervently for Chuck's recovery.

I spoke with them for about an hour. I comforted them and told them wonderful stories of the times Chuck and I had danced together and how positive, uplifting and supportive their father had always been.

I approached Chuck's bedside again. He was in a coma, which he had been in for over a week. He was on a respirator. His eyes were closed. His breathing was mechanically forced and labored. His body energy was colorless.

My intention was to relieve the fluid in his lungs, to strengthen him to the point he could breathe on his own, to restore – to his very young 62 years of age – the health and vitality I associated with him.

I touched him.

"Chuck, it's Liz Severino," I said softly, aloud. I flowed a strong current of Reiki energy into his body.

Although his son and daughter had told me Chuck hadn't responded to anyone or anything since entering the coma, his left eyebrow went up immediately and his face – even though the eyes stayed closed – brightened. *He knew it was me.*

"Chuck, I came to help heal you. I'd like your permission," I thought the words. We were connected, I knew thinking the words was enough.

What happened next was to become yet another exceptionally powerful lesson in dying and death.

"Let me go," he said telepathically. *"Release me. I've seen the other side, I've seen the Light. I want to go."* He was almost frantic with his plea.

"What do you want me to do?" I asked, confused. I was a Healer, I thought! I had come to heal! Do Healers let people die? Can dying be healing?

"Tell my son and daughter that I love them and that I want to go. I've seen the other side and I want to go. Tell them they've done enough. Please, Liz, tell them to stop praying for me to recover and stay with them, and to leave it in God's hands. And release me now."

I started to cry softly, tears slowly and steadily flowing down my cheeks. I was shaking.

"I release you. I love you, Chuck. Thank you for everything you've

always been for me and for the joy of dancing that you've always given to me. Go in peace."

Chuck's body trembled. A still energy I'd never experienced before filled him completely. He was waiting for something.

I turned to his son and daughter.

"Your father has asked me to thank you for your prayers. He loves you both. He's asked me to ask you to leave all in God's hands."

I couldn't speak the words that he wanted to go.

"Thank you, thank you," they both said, eyes tearing.

I prayed with them then embraced them both and went to Chuck, touching him one more time. His body was full of a strange mixture of anticipation and relief. It came to me suddenly and inexplicably to leave his hospital room.

"There are many definitions of healing," Guidance explained as I left the room. *"You must never be attached to a result. Always set your clear intention for what you'd like, ask for or speak it, but attach only to the Highest Good for All Concerned. And then, let it go."*

I continued to cry softly as I walked down the corridor, unsure of my destination and unsure of why I had suddenly left the room.

I soon found out that Chuck died right after I left his room. I learned how powerfully responsive our essence energy is to loving intention and prayer. I learned that we can want and choose death, including its precise timing.

My "own" near-death experience was not like those I've read about or listened to others describe. I'm sometimes overly sensitive to other people's thoughts and opinions; and I have been very select for years about speaking of it, because of this. I did not go through a tunnel. I was not met by those, animal or human, I have loved consciously while in form. Wall-clock time, I later learned, I was "dead" for about 10 minutes. It seemed much, much longer.

I did experience light so bright that I knew I would have been blinded by it in "normal" circumstances.

I was met by a committee. A committee of a dozen forms, presenting as human men and women, all of whom I instantly sensed were wise beyond my comprehension; who emitted love and compassion beyond anything I had felt to date in my conscious experience; who represented an eternity beyond my ability to conceive; and none of whom I recognized but all of whom I somehow knew.

The lead energy, who although I intuitively knew she was ancient, appeared as a healthy, late-middle-aged human adult. She spoke to me of "missions" and "choices." Much about human consciousness was taught by downloading energetic snap-shots of learning experiences completed.

I was invited to make a choice, to join them and work from the Essence Energy World already a part of their team, or to return to my physical body and work from form. I was again assured I was a part of their team, always, and would continue to be. Either way was fine with them; however, they informed me the impact would be stronger and more direct for human consciousness, if I returned to form and let their love and compassion work through me directly in the physical world. They explained they needed colleagues in form to make certain concepts and breakthroughs a reality in the world of form and physical vibration.

I remember asking why my experience was different from those I had learned about. I had expected to see animal and human loved ones I had known during my physical life.

I was told I was a worker-energy, that I volunteered for this, and that since I have many spirit guides and counselors, they met me first. They said I would experience the full, "normal" transition sequence at another time, that is, spirit guides first, then all the animals with whom I've shared love, and then all the humans. This will happen, they assured me, when my work is done and I will be met and gathered around with great celebration and joy.

I chose to return to form.

We choose life, too, I learned.

My experiences of death and dying and lessons continue. Most recently, in August of 2000, my Mother died; in May of 2001, my Step-Father (my Dad for 38 years) died, both therefore crossing over within 9 months of each other. My parents both consciously chose the peace and joy on the other side and an end to their physical lives here. They were prepared and both knew about six months before.

The day after my Mother died, her image presented in my conscious awareness. Radiant, peaceful, full of compassion, understanding, alert, appreciative, she was completely devoid of any negativity, judgement, ego, aggression or resentment. Her image was of her when about 30 years old, in the prime of her life, exquisitely beautiful, very happy, healthy, and very much at peace. Her personality, especially her twinkling eyes, was still quite evident.

The image of my Mom stayed in my consciousness for about five hours, teaching me about what happens when we leave form. I experienced a profound and infinite love. I understood again why some call this love "the peace that passes all understanding."

Agnes Sanford, an extremely powerful spiritual healer who once lived about 3 miles from me in Moorestown, NJ, used almost identical words when describing her father's visit to her after his passing. Wovaka, a revered Paiute shaman and messianic figure, chronicled in *"Through Indian Eyes: The Untold Story of the Native American Peoples,"* had a mystical experience in 1889 in which he described "throngs of deceased Indians engaged in their old-time sports and occupations, all happy and forever young."

One of the things my Mom taught was, there *is* a life review. For all creatures. It is much more extensive for humans and the animals who choose to share all or part of their lives with humans.

The words that presented in my mind while my image of my Mom was in my creative consciousness, recounted what her life review was like, the questioning, the process. The questions asked of her, in her review, seemed to fall into three categories:

How well did you get beyond fear?
How well did you serve others?
How well did you treat yourself?

In other words, *"How well did you learn to love?"*

These and many other experiences have added immeasurably to my understanding of this phase of the cycle of life. Each one has taught me something, given me some lesson of the energetics of or appreciation for dying and death and beyond. I've begun to notice a shift in my awareness, from fearing death and its aftermath, to accepting it, to having a deep appreciation for the essence energy life and what I now call, "The Other Side."

Death as a teacher, while I'm still in form. What a blessing!

About Rudy: Baron Rudolph Henrik Jacob von Knerr was our family dachshund. My Dad felt that a long dog needed a long name, and since this is a long chapter, well, it just seemed to fit! We are pictured here together in 1956. Rudy stayed with us, teaching us much about the joy of living, particularly the joy of escaping and adventuring, until shortly after my Dad's death, when my Mom felt forced to give him away because we moved into an apartment complex that didn't allow dogs. The receiving family were friends of my younger brother and we stayed in contact until Rudy's death several years later.

Grandmother Willow's Song

Listen with your heart,
You will understand.

Part II:

Essence Energies and Stages

Hippocrates

The soul is the same in all living creatures, although the body of each is different.

The Cycle of Life

Kantischna

*M*uch of the human fear of death seems to have three causes: the fear of the unknown; the fear of experiencing great suffering and pain during dying; and/or the fear of dying alone. I have further observed, that we tend to project these fears on others who are having a death or dying experience, including and particularly, our animal friends. These fears are the fears which I believe contribute to the extreme pain we feel as care-humans, in making euthanasia decisions for our animals.

I have also observed and experienced, that none of these fears is grounded. No single animal I have witnessed during death, nor even a human, has crossed over unaccompanied or unmet by essence energies. We do not separate from physical form alone.

Regarding pain, treatments from varying traditions have made great progress in its relief. When we experience great pain and suffering, it is my direct experience and confirmed by the medical model, that our consciousness escapes the pain at some point by distancing itself from the present circumstances of the physical body and by entering a different level of reality, a different level of consciousness. We therefore no longer feel the pain to the same extent. This separation and the beginnings of it are what I now know is behind the loss of body color I have frequently seen in humans or animals about to cross over.

As for the unknown, there are many near-death experiences from various traditions and cultures whose learnings are readily available to us. There are many of us now who talk to "the Other Side," whatever the original physical form. We can know now that consciousness and awareness continue, albeit with different frames of reference.

It comes to me to say, that I am now truly one who absolutely believes in the Divine Oneness, in Kinship with All Life.

I've shared with you that what people believe is important to me, particularly the various ways that people choose to acknowledge and worship their God(s). My religious history is, my birth Father was a Roman Catholic and my mother a Presbyterian. When they married, they blended their beliefs and became Episcopalian. I was raised and confirmed both Presbyterian and Episcopalian. I went to Quaker meetings and attended an Episcopalian school and College. My family employed household help who were Baptist. When my birth father died, my Mom remarried Episcopalian.

I live in a primarily Jewish neighborhood. My dog is named after a Cherokee Indian. I am ordained through and hold a Doctorate from the Universal Life Church. I am enrolled in the Spiritual Healer's Ordination Program of renowned Spiritual Healer, Dr. Ron Roth. I spent part of a summer with Hindu priests and healers in Bali and part of another summer in Mexico with Mayan shamans. I earned a second Doctorate in Religious Studies with a concentration in Healing Through Prayer and Touch, through the University of Global Religious Studies affiliated with the University of Missouri. I have studied at least fourteen languages and am currently learning Aramaic. A primary gift of mine this life-time is "Interpreter of Tongues." One way I use this gift, is as a healing communicator for people and animals.

I am blessed in that my Uncle Robert Patton, already mentioned as an animal communicator and hands-on healer, also first introduced me to St. Francis when I was a child. The teachings of St.

Francis have guided me my entire life. The Prayer of St. Francis has been my life-motto from the time I first read it.

I am also a bio-energy therapist and healer. I've spent years studying the Judao-Christian Kabbalah. I am actively taking classes through Michael Harner's Foundation for Shamanic Studies. I am a Teaching Reiki Master and have studied and received certifications in numerous other healing modalities, including Prana, Huna, Transform Breathwork, QiGong, and acupressure.

I am aligned with Sathya Sai Baba. I absolutely honor his message of Truth and Love.

Interestingly, I am also highly scientifically trained. I served IBM as a large computer architecture designer and through them earned a Masters in Computer Science and Business Administration. I worked on an IBM-confidential, international, hand-picked development team in the late 1960's which resulted in the design and development of the Universal Control Language that became one of the seed design strategies for what we know of now as the Internet.

At the time, virtually all computers used different architectures with vastly different interfaces. We were told by most, that what we intended to do was impossible. But our group of seven felt it was possible to create one interface that all computers could recognize; IBM funded us; and we did it, revolutionizing the potential of the way the computer industry looked at itself. The first book I wrote was *Guide to International Computer Systems Architecture.*

Listening to, experiencing, synthesizing and presenting various practical, blended viewpoints from the One, is a part of my being.

I never used to believe in "reincarnation" in any of the various forms that many world religions teach it. It was perfectly fine with me that others did. I knew that over 75% of the world's people, believe or even feel they outright *know* that "reincarnation" according to some definition, is real.

But the scientist in me hadn't really seen reincarnation, the endless life of the soul, or anything seemingly like it. So, still influenced by my primarily U.S. Christian up-bringing and my scientific training, I just didn't believe it, myself. Even *with a* Doctorate in Religious Studies. Or as some of my friends often quipped, *"Because of* a Doctorate!"

I experienced an epiphany in the late 1980's during which a miracle witnessed by 7 others saved my life. As I healed from that "accident," I started to experience direct knowings about healing myself and others. My intuitive abilities grew exponentially. I began to receive messages from human and animal bodies as to what the experience of the body was, and what it was asking for, in order to experience healing.

It never occurred to me that I would use my gift as an animal communicator, which I've had since birth, to help beyond the animals in my own household. But the "accident," the epiphany, the miracle, changed my life. The ability to communicate took a high profile position in my daily experience. I began to listen to the animals on behavior, emotional trauma, and physical health issues. Issues of healing. Issues of dying.

The animals have a VERY different "knowing" about death from the opinion of most humans in "Western" Civilization.

They absolutely know that death as humans know it is a decomposition of physical form only. Identifiable consciousness and awareness continue.

The animals know that the phenomenon humans call life has two components: that which we call physical form, primarily biochemical; and that which we in English often have no name for, which the animals call living consciousness, essence energy or aware-spirit. The animals know that these two aspects can exist separately, although only a few subsets of human cultures on our planet so far understand or acknowledge both of these aspects as forms of life.

The animals know that animating energy which we could call "Holy Spirit," or in Hebrew *ruach*, in Sanskirt *prana*, in Chinese *Chi*, in Japanese *Ki*, permeates matter and by penetrating it and choosing to live cooperatively with it, animates it. Death as humans know it, is its withdrawal, that is, the concentrated, identifiable essence energy leaves a physical form, after which humans would observe that medical signals such as EEG's and EKG's are no longer detectable.

After this withdrawal, the physical form starts to decompose and this is what many humans call death. Devoid of the essence energy, the wiring which surrounds and penetrates all cells of our body, the Universal energy initiates the subdivision of the physical body into the smallest of particles, which some call "dust."

The "wiring" of the essence energy holds the DNA and other intelligence for the physical body to which it belonged and also serves as a medium for the flow of information throughout the body and between the body and other bodies. The "wiring" is a structured subset of the bioenergy of the entire Universe. When the "wiring" or life energy leaves, the memory of the physical structure disappears, leaving only the living essence energy itself.

The animals know highly recognizable, concentrated aspects of their being, which I've come to call their essence energy, can align with a new wiring structure and take on or create a new physical form. This is what some call "reincarnate."

The animals' essence energies often even know and willingly communicate when, where, and into what form, they will re-present. They know no two physical forms are ever completely alike. Each "wiring" of an essence energy, when combined with a physical form, has a totally unique blueprint or energetic (vibrational) signature.

This my experiences with the animals have resoundingly confirmed. I have also noticed that human civilizations or cultures that believe in any form of reincarnation, feel far less fear of death of the physical body, than those who don't. Please note that this in no way demeans the sacredness of life in physical form. If anything, it increases it, because the physical form, however temporal, is truly recognized as the temple of the Divine Soul.

My first direct adult experience with an essence energy, separate from form, occurred in 1992, soon after I had become a professional animal communication consultant and energy healer. I had moved into a house in 1987 and discovered I had many crickets in my house and garage.

I decided I didn't like hearing the crickets' endless chirping inside my house. I felt concern for what rugs or other fabrics they might eat. I particularly didn't like seeing them jumping all over my kitchen floor when I visited for a late-night snack and suddenly turned on my kitchen light.

I created an agreement with the crickets that I would give them all the food and water they would like, in the garage; and they would not be visible or audible in my house, as long as I was physically in the house. I further informed them, that if they presented and my cocker spaniel saw them, that I would take that as a request for assistance in leaving form and I would let my cocker spaniel have his natural way with them.

This agreement worked flawlessly from 1987 to 1992. I would periodically find dead crickets in my house and I would gently collect their bodies and take care of them. If I made a quick visit to the garage, I would surprise them and I would often see dozens of them. But the garage wasn't part of the "no see, no hear" deal and I was okay with this.

One afternoon in 1992, I saw a particularly large cricket jump from underneath my family room couch directly into the line of vision of my cocker spaniel. I was startled. I knew the crickets knew the agreement, which had worked perfectly for years.

I quickly sent a reminder of the contract to the cricket, just as my cocker spaniel sat up. The cricket sent back an acknowledgment of the terms of the contract.

"Watch this," he stated simply.

I sent the contract reminder again. My cocker spaniel appeared to have cricket-snack on his mind.

"Watch this," the cricket repeated.

My cocker spaniel, Tanaka, pounced on the cricket, surprising me by playing with it more like a cat than a cocker spaniel. The cricket experienced wounding. It would die soon.

"Watch this," the cricket said again. *"Are you watching this?"* he demanded with a sense of urgency.

Tanaka seemed about to finish off the cricket. A flash of communication went between him and the cricket, like the data communications programs I had written as a computer systems programmer:

Tanaka: *"Food, death, now. Acknowledge."*

Cricket: *"Acknowledge. Teaching now."*

A remarkable thing happened. My cocker spaniel backed away from the cricket. A silvery-white form lifted from the physical body of the cricket itself. It moved above the physical body, slightly overlapping, still not quite separate.

"Are you watching this?" the cricket demanded of me.

"I'm watching," I sent.

The silvery-white form went back into the cricket-body for a fraction of a second then lifted higher, steadily separating completely from the physical form. It hovered above the physical form and then repeated this return and withdrawal.

"Watch me," it said. The awareness came from the silvery-white form, not the physical body form.

"You've just seen your first soul/spirit, the essence energy, separate from form," the cricket announced. *"The consciousness stays with the soul/spirit, the essence energy. I am still addressable to you."*

I watched Tanaka. He looked at me.

"We orchestrated this for you. Get it."

I felt the extraordinary difference in the subtle energies of the cricket body with the essence energy within it and the cricket body with the essence energy separated. The essence energy hovered in the air above the cricket body for a few seconds. It sent me the energy that it was satisfied with my attention and level of understanding. Then it raised several feet above the floor and disappeared from my perception.

♡   ♡   ♡

My first conscious experience with an animal whose essence energy had returned and taken another animal form, an animal essence energy I had first met in a different form, occurred shortly after the cricket experience. A wonderful lady, Carol W., in Cherry Hill, NJ had called me to consult for her cats, to determine why they were urinating all over her floors. When I arrived in Carol's home, her cats were quite ready to speak and told of anger and other feelings about events that had transpired in the house, all of which Carol confirmed.

Two cats in particular were urinating outside the litter box; the third was not. We resolved the situation, came to an agreement between the cats and Carol, and everything went pretty much as it normally does. Except that the third cat evidenced very unusual behavior during the session.

Usually when I do a consultation, all the animals who can, enter into the room I'm in. One particular house I did had 30 cats and ALL of them managed to somehow get into the living room with me when I was there, to their humans' (and my) amazement!

This doesn't happen, if the animal is running a scam of some sort. When an animal is running a scam with its human and doesn't want its scam to be uncovered as a result of my presence and questioning, the animal will usually go to the furthest corner it can, away from me, while watching me intently.

This cat didn't do either. He didn't enter the room. He didn't go to a corner and watch me intently. He sat quietly on the border between the living room and the dining room.

When I was done the consultation, I looked at Carol.

"Do you want me to sense your third cat?" I asked, quite curious.

"Who, Lucky? No, he's fine, there's no need to read him," she replied. "As a matter of fact, he's a gem."

"I'm curious. We're pretty much done, do you mind if I talk to him a little bit?"

"No, that's okay, go ahead."

I connected with Lucky. I asked him telepathically why he was neither in the room nor in a distant corner. I had never seen that behavior before.

"I've been waiting for you to finish. Do you recognize me?" he asked.

"Recognize you?" I replied. *"I've never seen you before. I've never been in this house before."*

"You're looking at my physical body," he said. *"Look closer,"* he coached. *"What do you see? Do you recognize me?"*

Suddenly I saw/felt a memory of a kitten in Deptford, NJ. I used to do healing touch demonstrations in all the pet stores in the Greater Philadelphia Area. On a Saturday in June, a mother and her daughter came early as I was setting up for a demonstration. The little girl was carrying a kitten. She offered me the kitten, crying, "Can you help him? What happened to him? Is he going to die?"

I accepted the kitten from her, instantly sensing that the kitten was dying. Almost every bone in its body was broken. As I telepathically asked the kitten what happened, the mother asked, "What happened? I think I know but I'm too distraught to say it."

The kitten showed me the energy of a young male, blond hair, wearing a plaid shirt. The young male had a baseball bat. The kitten showed me that the male wanted a baseball and didn't have one, so used the kitten's body instead.

"The kitten met up with a young male, blond hair, wearing a plaid shirt," I started.

"Craig!" (name has been changed) the little girl blurted out.

"He had a bat with him when we saw him last," the mother said.

I looked at the mother. Locking eyes with her, without

speaking, I nodded slowly. She started to cry.

"Daddy won't let us pay for any help. He says the kitten's going to die and no one can do anything about it," the little girl blurted out.

"Your Dad is probably right, your kitten is probably going to die," I replied simply. "But that doesn't mean you can't do anything."

"My daughter noticed the sign, that you were going to be here today, the healing touches. We were hoping that you could help. Is there anything we an do?"

She thought a moment. "Should we call the police on this boy?" the mother asked.

"It would be worth letting your local detectives know. Children who abuse animals often grow up to abuse humans."

I suddenly felt a surge of energy from the kitten. The energy I was receiving was the energy of compassion, of understanding, and of total forgiveness.

I was dumbfounded. I was prepared to be angered and judgmental over the boy's actions.

"Your kitten has no hostility towards this boy," I offered, taking my cue from the kitten and quickly draining my anger. "Perhaps it's best to take your cue from your kitten. Your kitten holds only compassion, understanding, and total forgiveness for this boy."

I surprised myself with my feeling and my words.

Both the mother and daughter were now crying. The mother said, "I so needed to hear this. There's other stuff going on, maybe you've already sensed that. I so needed to hear this. Thank you. Thank you. I really needed to see a powerful example of forgiveness."

"Thank your kitten," I said simply.

We talked about her options to ease the kitten's suffering. I gave her the name of a veterinarian I knew would help that day *pro bono*.

All of this, suddenly flashed into my eyes, as I stared at Lucky. *"Now do you know me?"* Lucky demanded.

"You're the kitten?" I asked, incredulous.

Lucky sent acknowledgment energy.

"I'm still forgiveness energy," he added.

"Carol!" I blurted out. "Does the energy of forgiveness have anything to do with your life right now?"

I was so excited at what was happening that I wasn't really paying attention to Carol. Sitting across the living room from me, Carol reacted as if I had hit her, physically falling back into her chair. She immediately started to cry. She told me of her husband suddenly walking out on her years before, of her anger and her pain. I listened to her, witnessed her, facilitated the soothing of her pain.

"Tell her my story," Lucky coaxed.

I told Carol what had just happened and how amazed I was. Lucky was the essence energy of the kitten, working the same energy, the energy of forgiveness. We spoke for quite a while.

Suddenly I found myself asking, "Carol, how did you get Lucky? Why did you call him Lucky?"

"You're not going to believe this!" she exclaimed. "It's a miracle this animal is still alive!"

She went on to explain that a close friend, Dave, worked in a factory in North East Philadelphia. One day as he was working he heard a loud thump against his entry door. He raced out and saw a car speeding away. Wondering at the sound, he soon found a paper bag. He turned to go back inside, then noticed the bag was moving from within. Gingerly he opened the bag. Inside it was a kitten.

Carefully he brought the kitten out of the bag. Although thrown with great impact against the door, it seemed okay ... no broken bones.

"This time!" I thought.

Dave named the kitten Lucky and brought it to Carol. Carol was delighted.

Lucky flashed me an energy of agreement with the story as Carol presented it. He seemed extremely amused at my observation,

"No bones broken, this time!" He was quite satisfied with himself.

"How did you think you got here?" he demanded.

Incredulous, I spoke the question to Carol. "Carol, how did you find me?"

"Elizabeth, you're not going to believe this!" she exclaimed. Pausing, she thoughtfully added, "Then again, maybe you will!"

Carol explained that on the day she called me, she had retrieved her mail and entered her kitchen with the mail in her arms. As she was walking across the kitchen floor, Lucky suddenly climbed up on top of the refrigerator, which she had never before seen him do, and dive-bombed her, sending the mail scattering from her arms in all directions.

In her mail that day, she had received a copy of the Associated Humane Society's *Humane News*. The little newspaper opened as it fell . . . to the center spread, which was advertising a fund-raiser for the Popcorn Zoo featuring me as a special guest, doing animal communication sessions as fund-raisers for the event. She thought of her problems with her two cats, got my number, and called me.

All through Lucky!

By the time we were done, Carol had healed from her earlier traumatic suffering. Thanks to Lucky. And I had an experience of the mystery of essence energies changing forms for the first time in my conscious awareness, and the extraordinary potential of the healing energy of that mystery.

About Kantischna: Kantischna, a black-and-white, blue-eyed Siberian Husky female was born on 29 January, 1989, in a little village called Yterraenger, Sweden. She transitioned in Arloev, Sweden, on 19 February, 2000. In April, 2000, her loving care-humans asked me to communicate with her. Her spirit presented and among other things told us she was planning on reuniting with her care-humans, Gunvor and Jurg, in their current life-time. She told us her plan was to be born in a litter whose puppies would be available in August. The litter, she said, would be located within 90 kilometers from her care-humans' current home in Sweden and furthermore, that a name associated with the litter would contain a "Ber" and "ng" sound.

We explained to her that Gunvor takes holiday in weeks 1 to 3 in August and that there was a risk of Gunvor not finding the litter if she were away and that Gunvor would be in deep despair over this. Kantischna then agreed to be born earlier, in order to be available at the end of July. She was clear that the signs that it was she would be her distinct body markings as well as the obvious traits of personality.

Although Gunvor was quite concerned she would not find Kantischna and knew of no breeders or kennels in the area Kantischna mentioned, one did come to light in July. The letter "B" was in the name of the person owning the male (from Germany). The name of the owner of the kennel where she was born was Henning, which, Gunvor wrote, when visualized could be very well taken for Berning. There was a complication in that the kennel owner loved the energy of the new puppy, feeling it was the strongest, and wanted to keep it. Many extra prayers for the Highest Good were said. The owner came to fall in love with and want a different puppy and was very happy with that new choice. Now as Archtika, Kantischna's essence energy and Gunvor are delightedly together again.

Henry Beston

We need another and a wiser and perhaps a more mystical concept of animals. Removed from universal nature and living by complicated artifice, man in civilization surveys the creatures through the glass of his knowledge and sees thereby a feather magnified and the whole image in distortion. We patronize them for their incompleteness, for their tragic fate for having taken form so far below ourselves. *And there in do we err*. For the animal shall not be measured by man. In a world older and more complete than ours, they move finished and complete.

Cedar

The Animals Speak

*D*esert Dan once said, *"There's opinions about animals, and there's facts about animals. If you want opinions, ask the humans. If you want the facts, ask the animals."*

So, what is the animals' viewpoint on euthanasia? Do they ever invite it or not? And if they do invite it, is there a time that it is better for them? If so, under what circumstances and how can we know?

As of this writing, I've communicated with tens of thousands of animals in 23 countries. In person. One at a time. In groups. In multi-animal households, singly and collectively. At seminars, workshops, presentations, animal communication gatherings, charity events and animal parties. Over the telephone. Via the Internet. Via the Etheric-Net.

Many of the animals have been suffering. Many have been elderly and infirm. Many have been in extremely compromised health, in varying stages of dying.

I've "stayed with" many of them, giving healing energy, sometimes helping with transitions. More often, I've consulted on what they feel they need to return to health, collaborating with their care-humans and their health professionals, communicating their view of their reactions to various interventions or therapies.

Many animals have lived. Others have been euthanized. Still others have died peacefully and naturally at home with their care-humans. Many have orchestrated their own deaths.

I've noticed when there is an honoring of the animal, an honoring of all phases of the process of death, the energy feels very different. This includes rescue animals who by virtue of their extreme frustration with being in human companionship or inability to be socialized in a way safe for human companionship, have demonstrated behaviors requiring euthanasia; or unwanted animals who by virtue of abandonment or owner decision are euthanized.

Interestingly, all of the animals who have left form, who have transitioned, where I have been involved, have asked their humans for some form of ritual, however brief, honoring their passage.

I now also receive communications from spirit/souls. I listen to spirit/souls in living bodies, human and animal; and I also listen to them when they've crossed over or are incorporeal.

Looking back, I can see a lifetime of preparation to be able to understand and communicate their viewpoint on this topic.

About Cedar: Cedar is an Irish Wolfhound living in British Columbia. He has the infinite wisdom and depth of his breed plus the love and respect of many care-humans. He is also a teacher who among other things, has shared the correct positions for Reiki touch healing for his breed.

The Three Stages

Rune

*L*ive in a manner supporting that when at all possible, let an animal or a human live and die with grace and honor, in balance and order, with all due respect to the various health approaches possible, with as little invasion of their bio-spirit as possible and as much reverence as possible. I believe my birth Father, my Mother, my Step-Father, and many others, consciously chose the timing of their deaths. It has occurred to me that at some level, it is possible we all do.

I have further noticed that in almost all cases, regardless of the stage of death, the essence energy, that is, the living consciousness and awareness, stays with or around the physical body for a limited period of time immediately after it separates from the physical form. It is quite present during the first few days and week, and usually disappears and presents again at intervals sometime during the first year. Its departure from form completes the death of the physical body and initiates its decomposition. What happens after that varies.

I've known for years that some essence energies or spirits, after this initial period of time, were clear very quickly; and that some seemed to be quite confused, for long periods of time, before I could effectively communicate with them for more than a few seconds. Some spirits I have sensed, mostly human suicides, are confused and apologetic even when sensed years later.

But I haven't known why. The animals have answered these questions.

The animals tell me there are three stages of death. They call these stages, rather simply, Stage 1, Stage 2, and Stage 3.

Killing a living creature and ending a physical life has very different consequences during and after the death of the physical body depending on two primary factors. The first is the stage of death that the living body is in. The second is the energy of intention or spiritual attention around the death of the physical form and the separation of the two life forms, that is, the life form of the physical body and the life form of the essence energy.

The differences seem to come down to the ability or lack thereof of the physical body to recover, including the amount and the length of time of the physical suffering; and the amount of time and the approach, meaning the energetic environment or spiritual attention, the living essence energy of consciousness has experienced or has had a chance to experience, in preparing for its separation from living (dying) form, including the degree and extent of any attachment to anything or anyone in the physical world, that the essence energy was experiencing.

If you "kill" a living creature too soon, too quickly, when the physical body and/or the spirit-body are not ready yet, not even in any of the stages, meaning still quite attached to form, and without any spiritual acknowledgment, preparation or attention, then the spirit/soul becomes extremely confused. It becomes stunned. It may not even know it is "dead." It can take a long time, six months to 2 years or more, human time, before it becomes clear.

Killing an animal in such a manner before the 1st stage of death has even begun and without any spiritual acknowledgment or attention results in this extended confusion. This could mean that an animal which was otherwise healthy was killed by accident or intention. Please note that this does not seem to happen when a perfectly healthy animal dies by its own conscious choice, for example, in heroic action or because it simply chooses to change forms. Nor does it seem to happen when a perfectly healthy creature loses its life to become food either for another animal or for a human and is honored in the process the way animals in most aboriginal cultures are honored.

Mark was a formerly traumatized dog taken from an abusive

environment to an animal rescue farm. He had bitten over a dozen times. He had stopped the biting behavior while on the rescue farm, yet as soon as he was placed into a loving adoptive home, he bit again and was returned to the farm.

In consultation Mark was quite clear he distrusted humans and no longer wanted to be around them, except those on the farm. He had figured out that if he bit anyone in his adoptive homes he would be returned to the farm, which is where he wanted to be. It was not possible for him to stay on the farm, however, because the farm was at its limit for animals it could keep. When he understood this, he asked immediately for euthanasia, stating his desire to come back as a wild animal in no direct contact with humans. His humans granted his request with appreciation and ceremony.

A few months later awareness of him took over my consciousness. He let me know he was happily living as a squirrel in the woods of the very farm whose energy he wanted to be near.

In the 1st stage of dying the physical body of an animal can still recover. Even though the animals call it the "1st stage of dying", the animal actually knows that its physical body is capable of healing. Often it can heal itself while still requiring some cooperation from its immediate environment. The nature of the universe is towards wholeness and healing.

This cooperation would include proper food, rest, cleanliness of wounds or abrasions and perhaps some health care or veterinary intervention. An animal euthanized in the 1st stage and without spiritual preparation will be confused for anywhere from 6 to 12 months, human time.

In the 2nd stage of dying an animal's physical body may or may not recover. An animal in this stage knows it requires intervention of some sort in order for its physical body to heal. It is no longer able to heal itself and often will ask for help. An animal euthanized in the 2nd stage and without spiritual preparation will be confused for anywhere from 4 weeks to 6 months, human time.

Frick-Frack was an 8-1/2 year old cat. He was experiencing tumors in his jaw and throat. He was receiving therapy and interventions from his care-human and his veterinarian. In our consultation, Frick-Frack said he was not ready to transition. He said that he expected to live for many months longer in a relatively stable condition. He further stated that under no circumstances should he be given any procedure that involved general anesthesia.

About six months after this consultation, his care-human called me. Frick-Frack had died the month before during exploratory surgery. She was devastated, remembering Frick-Frack's caution and feeling terrible that she had allowed herself to be talked into disregarding that caution. Frick-Frack wasn't clear yet and wasn't ready to communicate at the time of her contact, so we opened again to him about two weeks' later. Frick-Frack advised us that his lungs were full of microscopic tumors and the anaesthesia had caused his body to experience failure. His human then remarked that two of three veterinarians had seen evidence of tumors in Frick-Frack's lungs, but the third, who had done the surgery, had not. I suggested that his care-human perform a spiritual ritual for Frick-Frack, which she agreed to do.

In the 3rd stage of dying an animal knows its physical body can no longer be healed without Divine intervention. It begins the separation of living soul/spirit from form. It has time to move between the earth and the etheric, time to prepare for the transformation and separation. When the final separation occurs, the etheric plane is by then familiar again, and there's much less, if any, shock. Often an animal will ask for euthanasia in this stage. Frequently, the animal will orchestrate the circumstances of its transition. Some animals are quite clear that their primary experience, from entry into the 3rd stage on, will be pain and progressive failure of the body. Many of them know they absolutely do not want continual or additional testing, surgeries, interventions, or therapies. Almost all of them know the joy and freedom they will be experiencing after they've left form. Many take care of their care-humans in very beautiful ways at this sensitive time.

Divine Intervention, in my experience, happens through either or both of two situations. First, an individual connected with Divine energy, for example, a spiritual healer, consciously invokes that energy (prays, decrees, performs healing touch) on behalf of the animal. Second, a very enlightened veterinary health professional (including a health professional who has been prayed for), becomes inspired with a sudden knowing and the resultant intervention or therapy reverses the animal's situation relative to its physical health.

I have on several occasions been the vessel for bringing healing prayer energy into situations reversing physical situations. I am also privileged to know wonderful veterinarians who are Inspired in their work.

The spirit/soul of an animal euthanized in the 3rd stage can be sufficiently clear to be contacted almost immediately and is usually completely clear in 2 to 6 weeks, human time.

An animal communication colleague tells of a horse who had undergone many tests and interventions. For months, the horse fiercely fought any approach by a veterinarian intent on euthanasia. One day the animal's energy changed. Tired of testing and interventions, he recognized the veterinarian's van, walked up to him and put his head down. He wanted to be released. He was clear in about six weeks.

Sleepy was a 21-year-old Beagle. He had been with his care-human, Fred, throughout his entire life. Mostly, Sleepy was an outside dog. Fred had constructed a wonderful dog-house for him, complete with insulation and shingled roof. Sleepy was very happy.

Sleepy knew, however, that it would be extremely difficult for Fred when Sleepy crossed over. He made the decision to leave his body when Fred was away. Sleepy waited almost a year for the appropriate time. When Fred left for Korea for an extended business trip, Sleepy knew he had his chance. He dug out of the back yard, a behavior he hadn't evidenced in many years. He managed to get himself taken into a household and hidden by a neighborhood boy suffering a very unusual infectious disease.

The boy's mother eventually realized Sleepy was hidden in her son's room and took appropriate action. It was too late for Sleepy. Sleepy's internal organs were not capable of withstanding the infection and deterioration. He was euthanized by the attending veterinarian to ease his suffering.

When I contacted Sleepy's essence energy after Fred returned, Sleepy was quite clear. He stated that he had orchestrated the entire event to save Fred the suffering of being with him or watching him die, which Sleepy felt was a pain too great for Fred to bear.

Casey was a formerly abused inner-city dog rescued at age 2 and adopted by a loving older couple who helped nurse him back to health. Residual behavior from his previous abuse included that Casey would sometimes lose control of himself and his awareness of his loving surroundings. When this happened he would bite at anything coming near his head or face, including his beloved care-humans. He was always extremely remorseful after these incidents. Working with a dog trainer made no substantial difference in his behavior and neither did working with an animal behaviorist or an animal psychologist. The recommendation was made to euthanize Casey. The care-humans called me.

In consultation with Casey, he told me he was experiencing weaknesses and pressures in his head which had been caused by severe blows to his head during his inner-city experiences. He said the attacks had always come from one particular direction and from one particular human. He pointed out that he only bit when someone approached him from that particular direction and that was because his re-activated fear blinded him and caused him to instinctively and violently defend himself.

His humans agreed that this was so. I asked his care-humans if they would be willing to be extremely alert and simply never approach Casey quickly from that direction and angle and they said they would.

They did what they said, honoring their contract, and Casey only bit twice more in his life, both times when he was asleep and then awakened suddenly and approached from the trauma-triggering angle.

Casey started to evidence a cancer experience when he was 11 years' old. As he approached his 12th birthday it was clear he was suffering, losing weight and appetite. When asked what his sign would be, he said he would do two things, so that in case his loving care-humans missed the one sign, they would pick up on the other. Firstly, he said he would lose all fear of being approached from his former trauma angle; and secondly, he would whimper-talk to his humans, looking at them deeply and asking them to relieve his suffering, a behavior he had never demonstrated in his almost 10 years with them.

Casey subsequently did both of these things. His care-humans assembled and honored Casey in a beautiful and joy-filled ritual and Casey's veterinarian assisted his crossing over. Casey contacted me about a month later and spoke of his great love for his care-humans, especially for their patience and compassion. He mentioned that his primary care-human's husband, who had transitioned a year before, met him when he crossed over and he was again enjoying his human's music.

Rune was a very energy aware Lhasa Apso truthful to his origins in antiquity as a monk's companion. He shared his most recent life with a very energy aware care-human. Rune had experienced several years with paralysis of his hind legs. His care-human needed to carry him outside and prop him up and hold him while he eliminated.

One autumn, Rune's care-human thought she had seen a sign of entering 3rd stage and called me for a consultation. Rune had been experiencing a down-turn in his apparent physical well-being. His care-human wondered if it was indeed time to help him leave form.

Rune had taken his Booda Bone into his bed, a behavior his care-human had never seen before. She was concerned.

When I consulted with Rune, however, he said he knew that euthanasia was on his care-human's mind and he wanted to let his care-human know that he wanted to stay in form. He therefore had taken an obvious item of play, indicating life, to his bed with him. Rune wanted to stay in form. It wasn't time yet. He returned to a stable state soon after this consultation.

In mid-April 2001 Rune was 15-1/2 years old. His care-human again called me for a consultation. Rune's physical body had taken a turn for the worse. His care-human was involved in 24-hour-a-day care-taking and was experiencing great strain. She also loved him dearly and wanted what was best for him.

Rune reminded us that he had orchestrated his healing before and would orchestrate his own transition. He said he thought he would be able to go on his own, but it looked to him now, that unless a major catastrophe befell him, he would ask for assistance in six weeks. He specifically told his human he would be transitioning over Memorial Day weekend. He privately told me that his care-human would need that time to get herself emotionally prepared and that he loved her dearly and would stay in form until that time.

His care-human was very upset and wanted to know if there was anything she could do. Rune asked specifically for esoteric healing and other energy modalities, including Reiki, which his energy-aware care-human knew. His human granted his request. Rune stabilized and experienced reduced suffering.

The next six weeks were good ones for him. He spent loving time with his care-human during the energy treatments and his care-human became more accepting of his eventual separation from form. She even began to doubt Rune's self-expressed time-table.

Rune had said his signs would be, he would bite his human twice and stop eating. Mid-week of Memorial Day weekend, he demonstrated both behaviors. We asked and Rune replied, "It's time." His care-human took him to her veterinarian. Rune said that his care-human was giving him life supporting energy and that she would need to stop the procedures now in order for his body to take it's natural course. The veterinarian and Rune's care-human decided all energy procedures would be stopped.

Rune's physical body deteriorated dramatically over the next two days. He was euthanized at his request that weekend, Memorial Day Weekend.

About six weeks later, Rune's spirit presented. He had cleared and he had a message.

The passage from this side to the other side is a very significant event in the lives of all concerned. It is often traumatic for those on this side and a major event of change and rebirth of the spirit, as spirit separates from form, for those moving to the other side. It's very common for the animals to want to talk about what happened around or during the time of their departure.

Consistent with his status as a very elevated spirit, Rune wanted to express his appreciation. First, he was very grateful and wanted to thank his human, especially to let her feel his love and know he was okay. Secondly, he wanted to thank his veterinarian.

Rune sent the following message through for the veterinarian who helped with his transition:

"Thank you for making my transition so easy and special. You bring great loving energies to the process of transition and all of us animals, whom you have helped, are deeply indebted to you. We serve you in Spirit. The easy and gentle flow with which I left my body, allowed me the energy to float freely and then I was gone."

Bud was a 12-year-old Golden Retriever. He had fallen and crushed three of the vertebrae in his back. He was partly paralyzed but still very much in a good and loving mood most of the time. He had an appetite and wanted to play even though his mobility was quite limited. Acupuncture and herbs helped him tremendously and he started to recover.

He fell again and this time became mostly paralyzed. He said he wasn't sure if his body would respond well this time to acupuncture and herbs but that it would be very clear around the second or third visit to the veterinarian. If there was not clear improvement at this time, Bud said, he wanted assistance in leaving form.

His veterinarian and care-human called me on a Thursday evening while Bud was in the office for his third visit. There was no improvement. Bud was in great pain whenever he tried to move his head and neck down to eat. He could no longer move without assistance. It was time, he said, to be released. His care-human brought him home, assembled Bud's and her loving care-humans and performed a beautiful ritual. The following morning, early, she took Bud to the veterinarian. This just happened as I write this and Bud is still in the early stages of separation.

I find this same process and staging of clearings after transitioning is also true of human consciousness. My best friend's mother suffered with Alzheimer's for years. She was clear within an hour of the death of her physical body.

I remember this experience well. I was working on my computer and at 12:30 that Thursday afternoon, awareness of her completely took over my consciousness.

The awareness said, "The phone's going to ring shortly. It'll be Jim, telling you I've crossed over. Please tell him I was working the energy of Gentle Grace this life-time and it is my intention to do that next life-time, too. Tell him I am at peace and I love him eternally."

The phone rang. It was Jim telling me his Mother had died. I passed along his Mother's message.

When my own Mother died in August of 2000, awareness of her came into my consciousness for over 5 hours the day after she crossed over. When she presented that day, she was already totally clear. She explained that since she had experienced pain and suffering for over 40 years, including 26 major surgeries, she had long ago begun the separation. It was the first time in my life that I experienced for a sustained period of time the mixture of joy, peace, and bliss that appears to be the reality of experience on the other side. Mother chose the timing of her death. Although the death certificate read "pneumonia," the cause was "choice."

My former husband's great-uncle was 96 when he crossed over. He called for my then-husband and myself and told us he had decided to die in three weeks, on a Thursday. He said he had decided he had lived long enough and he was tired. He asked us to let everyone know and to have his daughter call for last rites that Thursday morning.

We did. He had a chance to say "Good-bye" to everyone. He experienced last rites on that Thursday morning, as he had wanted. After lunch that Thursday he went to his bedroom to take a nap, went to sleep, and died. His energy was the energy of perfect peace.

About Rune: Rune was a Lhasa Apso with a wonderful and very elevated spirit. He and his contributions to our understanding are discussed extensively in this chapter.

Andrew Linzey

I hope that in all our activities of protest, persuasion, and advocacy, we never lose the insight that every creature has its own mysterious life that graces us with its presence.

Ajax

Signs of the Third Stage

The energy of humans or creatures who have died naturally or by conscious choice is very, very similar to the energy of animals euthanized in the 3rd stage. It is almost the same for them as dying naturally.

Human words cannot do justice to the extraordinary range, the difference, the distinctions, the continuum from the exquisite peace and joyful clarity of the subsequent essence energy of an animal euthanized in the 3rd stage with spiritual attention, to the painful, explosive confusion of an unprepared living creature leaving form even before the 1st stage and with no spiritual attention. Nor can human words appropriately stress how extraordinary it is and how important it is to know that the 3rd stage is so similar in its spiritual impact to natural death or death by conscious choice or spiritual agreement.

There are clues, behaviors, signs, and symbols that old, infirm, suffering, or terminally ill animals give us so that we can know when they are in the 3rd stage. Paying attention to these symbols allows us to euthanize them in a time that works for them, if they wish assistance in leaving form.

I again remember and acknowledge the animals who quite literally gave their lives in many ways and in all the stages so that I could understand the stages and their distinctions, energetically. I honor their deep command that I share this understanding. I remember the animals so clearly as I am now sitting at my computer writing this, that I am experiencing tears, yet again.

In one incredible week, toward the end of this painful and tear-filled period of experience and growth in my understanding, when I first was learning about the three stages, amazingly, every veterinarian with whom I collaborate, somehow, suddenly had a reason to contact me. I was able to tell them what I am now writing for you; and every one of them medically understood exactly what I was saying. Each confirmed they had noticed the presentation of one or more of the signs in animals in the 3rd stage, ranging from the disappearance of vital life force energy from the eyes; what is called delusional behavior; the ambient energy of pleading to be released from pain; marked changes in behavior, including no longer wanting to eat; and others.

A suffering animal friend's entry into the 3rd stage is marked by a sudden change in behavior, a change dramatic enough and different enough so that its care-humans notice. Please note we are talking about suffering, dis-eased, or old and infirm animals. An animal who has never bitten, may bite. An animal who has never experienced seizures, will experience fits. An animal which has never "sounded" excessively (barked, screeched) will sound excessively. *(Major Exception: an elderly cat doing what I call vocalizing is doing something VERY different . . . it is NOT an indicator of 3rd stage, it is healing itself. You can help it immensely if you react also in a healing manner, however, this is the topic of another book).* An animal which has always been familiar will become distant. An animal with normally bright eyes will present eyes distant and dimming. An animal formerly resistant to approach by a veterinarian in the intent to euthanize will submit to and in some cases gratefully approach the veterinarian, visibly requesting such assistance. Some animals simply want to stop all forced medicants, testing, poking, and prodding.

An animal formerly appearing to be quite profoundly aware of its environment will start to react in a manner reflecting perceptions or visions of essence energies not easily perceptible to average human senses. Such an animal, either entering into or already in the 3rd stage, may suddenly start to react as if it were (in human terms) delusional, relating to and or responding to figures that to human eyes "aren't there." What's happening at this point is that the animal's consciousness, its living essence energy, its vibrational resonance, is elevating due to the process of separation from physical form and it is actually starting to more clearly see and openly respond to energies, sometimes incorporeal human or animal and often called angelic, which most human eyes can't readily see. This happens with humans, too.

Please remember as you read these words on the stages, the normal quality of life signs. These include being mildly active, being interested in food, drink, sleeping, and what's going on around them, appearing comfortable and free of major pain and having control of their organs of elimination.

The deterioration of quality of life often occurs over an extended time and the passing of stages may not be obvious. And then again, they can be.

Babbit the Rabbit was two years old. He was experiencing a jaw diseased by cancer and was feeling poorly. One Sunday, his eyes glazed and he bit his human twice. She called me immediately.

Babbit the Rabbit said in his consultation that he was extremely remorseful for biting his care-human. It was a big deal to him that he had bitten her and he felt terrible about it. He said his jaw hurt tremendously sometimes for brief periods and that his head experienced dizziness at that time. He said he lost awareness and when he lost awareness, he bit. He said that he would lose awareness again and he would again become violent. He affirmed that his physical body could not sustain harmonious life and asked both for euthanasia and a passing ritual. His care-human accommodated both his wishes.

Breeze was a 17-year-old cat who was having a squamous cell carcinoma experience. His energy aware care-human offered him Reiki and comfort as often as possible. He wanted food but could not eat it on his own because his tongue was involved. He was very frustrated and often bleeding would occur after attempts to eat by himself. His human carefully fed him from a syringe.

His care-human called me after a particularly bloody episode. Breeze told me his body could no longer heal and that shortly he would be ready for assistance in leaving form. He would steadfastly refuse the syringe, he said, and that was how his care-human would know it was time. A few days later, he did exactly as he said he would.

Shawn was a 16-1/2-year-old dog who had shared his life with one primary human. Shawn could no longer walk and could no longer eliminate without assistance. In consultation with his care-human, Shawn said he was in constant pain and it was time to receive assistance in leaving form.

Bodie was a 14-year-old dog who was losing function. In our consultation he told us the integrity of his internal organs was failing and he was losing the mobility in his rear leg. He was very clear he would have several signs for his human: firstly, his would lose his appetite; secondly, he would experience loss of his urinary and bowel control; thirdly, he would evidence a moaning sound which would steadily increase; and fourthly, his leg would fail completely. It would be clear at that time, he told us, that his "bad" days would be outnumbering his "good" days. He further advised us that he wanted all "pushing and prodding" to stop. He anticipated that the playing out of the body's energetics of deterioration to the point of wanting assistance in leaving form would take three to four weeks. His human advised me later than three weeks to the day, all the signs evidenced.

Betty Boop was a 7-year-old dog of pure love. Her energy-aware care-human did Reiki and other holistic modalities for her to supplement veterinary attention, yet she responded to nothing. Her care-human's veterinary cardiologist indicated that little could be done although extra testing might reveal something. In our consultation she said that her heart was about to fail, that her physical body could not heal, that she wanted no additional testing, and that she would die quietly within the week in her care-human's home. Since her care-human was considering putting her in the veterinary hospital for the testing, she asked me to ask him to please wait a few days, so that they could be together. When I spoke this to her care-human he affirmed that he had sensed she was close, that as much as he didn't want this result, it was consistent with the deep knowing in his heart.

He did as she wished. He took off from work and stayed with her. Three days later she died beautifully in his arms.

Jean Marie was a hedgehog who was just entering third stage when her care-human contacted me. Jean Marie said she was very close indeed, but not just yet. She said that the day she refused a meal worm was the day she would be hurting inside with no possibility of cessation of pain and would then want help leaving form. Two days later she refused a meal worm. She felt very complete inside as she asked for assistance in leaving form.

Mable was a 12-year-old Schnauzer having a cancer experience. She was experiencing difficulty breathing, a constantly stuffy nose, and a loss of balance. She said she was close to entering 3rd stage but not there yet. Her sign, she said, is that she would start to throw up and nothing would relieve this. Two days later, she started to throw up, and nothing her care-human or veterinarian did was able to relieve it. Her care-human recognized her sign and requested assistance with euthanasia.

A lady sent the following email:

"Recently my oldest daughter had to help her best buddy Mischa, a black lab, pass over. Mischa was on medication for seizures, but over time, she was experiencing seizures anyway because the medication stopped working. She was not her loving self anymore and was in a stupor most of the time. My youngest daughter works for a vet, is trained in Reiki, and is able to communicate with animals. We all talked about the situation. It was an agonizing decision.

"We talked to Mischa the night before we took her to the Vet. We told her how much we loved her and thanked her for all her companionship that she gave to us. We took Mischa to the vet the following morning and held her while the medication was taking effect. We could see Mischa's essence energy leave her body. We saw her surrounded with golden light. She was so happy to be relieved of her body. Later that same day I checked in to see how she was and the same great joy was still running through her. We could all see in her eyes that this was a correct decision for her, and this was very comforting."

The following from a lady in Tasmania may capture this experience of loving care-humans best:

"Elizabeth, it has been a very emotional week. My beautiful Majesty cat who was 17 ½ years old became very sick last Saturday and she spent two days in the hospital on IV fluids but when she came off the drip she went down hill very fast. The blood test confirmed kidney failure and I had to make a decision about what to do on Tuesday afternoon.

"I totally loathe being in this situation because I have mixed feelings about putting an animal to sleep. Is it really my decision? Do I really have the right? The alternative was 4 days in the hospital for Maj on a drip which she hated; she wouldn't be here with us during that time and the chance of her dying at the clinic in a cage at night by herself was not an option in my mind.

"I made the decision to let her go and tried to get her vet to come to our home, but they were so booked at the clinic we had to travel up there. My son and both daughters were here at the time and we all went with Majesty and cuddled her. I held her in my arms for the final injection.

"My daughter came up with the idea of having Maj cremated and I was so thrilled she came up with this because I was beyond thinking or making any more decisions.

"Please tell me something. All the animals who died a natural death have been back to see me normally in a very short time of going over, but the ones who have been 'helped' at the end seem either very distant or I haven't seen them. I haven't seen Maj yet and am fretting about this in case my decision was wrong and did I cause her trauma in the spirit world?"

In my consultation with Maj, Maj advised that the clinic was over four hours away. Maj and the others had simply stayed awhile before making their way back.

If you're a care-human for a suffering or infirm animal, are beginning to be convinced your animal's physical body cannot recover, and suspect but aren't sure if your animal is in the 3rd stage or wants the assistance of euthanasia, ask your animal. A beautiful way of asking your animal is in the last section of this book.

If you're not sure of the answer, there are several things you can do. One is to notice that number of "really good" days your animal is experiencing compared to the "really bad" days. When days get to be mostly "bad" it's probably time to ask again. You can also ask yourself, "What are the motives here?" A gentle choice with spirit behind it will benefit all.

Repeat the procedure and this time, ask, "Will you please give me a sign, a clear behavior change, if and when you become ready, or if and when you enter the 3rd stage and when you're ready?"

The animals will always respond "Yes" to this question. They will always have a sign.

Then you pay attention. Marshall your awareness.

If you're still not sure, again repeat the procedure, and add, "Will you please make it very obvious if you're in or when you've entered the 3rd stage and when you're ready?"

Either your animal will show you a specific, easily-recognizable sign; or a series of specific, easily-recognizable signs; or you'll experience a profound knowing in your body; or you'll have a dream with a clearly interpreted message. Some people report hearing a voice. Others see a symbol with a clear message.

A beautiful ritual to ask for help in making your decisions appears in the last section of this book.

The clearer an animal's essence energy gets, the sooner it can move its essence energy on if it wants to. In many cases over my years as an animal communicator, animals have told their humans whether or not their primary essence energies would be together again in their human's current lifetime; and if so, have told the humans the geographical location, the approximate timing, and the form or species, in which their essence energies would present. Many are indeed now together again.

If this relates to your life, to the animals in your care, please know that the animals are OK with assistance in dying. It's easier on them ultimately, however, if euthanizing is done in the correct time and with an energy of spiritual attention.

About Ajax: *Ajax, a Norwegian Hedgehog having an experience of Wobbly Hedgehog Syndrome, was quite clear he wanted to stay with his loving care-human, Bobby, who had helped rescue him, until two behaviors evidenced. Firstly, Ajax said, he would become incontinent; and secondly, he would lose mobility in his fourth (back left) limb, rendering him immobile. He was quite clear that although his appetite and good mood would continue it would be time, when these two behaviors evidenced, to assist him in leaving form. After Ajax passed, Bobby took Ajax to a beautiful local cemetery supporting the non-profit organization, The International Association of Pet Cemeteries. He was very comforted that they were willing to do the cremation while he waited. He writes: "That felt so much better than having him "shipped off" to some other location." For more information and to find a pet cemetery/crematorium in your area:* http://www.iaopc.com.

A Spiritual Ritual

Oliver with Fred and Liz

Virtually every animal I've assisted at the time of crossing over has asked for a ritual honoring and assisting its spirit's separation from form. Many animals have requested that specific people be present and/or that specific items be included, especially pictures and bedding or favorite play-items. In my experience the animals have considered the needs of spirit, their beloved care-humans, and their own specific needs in their requests for such honoring rituals.

The process of death and the efforts of a care-human at the time of dying and death transcend all religions and philosophies. Appropriate action will always come from the knowing deep within your own heart. Trust your heart while remembering Reverence for All Life.

The simplest ritual involves assembling in an appropriate location, selected care-humans who have played a part in your animal's life, other animal friends still in form, pictures or physical belongings of the animal to be honored, and a white candle. The care-humans would be the humans who most enjoyed your animal friend along with you during your animal friend's life. Usually this includes the humans most significant in your life and theirs.

The other animal friends still in form, would be any animals who live in your house, farm, or stable, or any animals with whom your animal regularly socialized or whom your animal enjoyed.

The pictures would be pictures that would show joy or stories of personality or remembrance. The physical belongings would be the belongings most used by or most present with the animal, having its energy, for example, a collar, leash, bridle, or favorite toy.

Under the best of circumstances your animal will still be in form when you perform this honoring ritual. It is never too late, however. If it comes to you to do an honoring ritual for an animal or animals already transitioned, regardless of the date or even the number of years, do it.

Invite as many animal friends as possible and preferably all of the animal friends living in the household. The animals know nature has no favorites, loving all creatures equally. They know each living thing must learn to responsibly exercise its right to draw resources from life. They accept the reality of ultimately relinquishing form in order to nourish the Earth and return to the larger, everlasting system. They have a deep knowing that spirit must be honored. It is exceptionally soothing and encouraging for them to see their care-humans engaged in ritual honoring of a transitioning or transitioned essence energy.

I did a group animal communication session once in a very small grooming room in a very large pet store. We thought about six people would attend yet twenty-two animals and their humans crowded into that incredibly small room. Humans without animals volunteered to leave the room to stand in the open door-way.

One human had brought his animal for a reading because it was showing all the signs of extreme grief and despair. He wanted to know why.

When I connected with the animal and questioned it gently, I learned that this animal's life-long animal companion had died. It was distraught. No one had told it what had happened that had caused the death or what had happened to its friend's body. There had been no acknowledgment, nothing. One day, this animal's friend had left the house and had never come back.

The human confirmed that nothing had ever been said to the grieving animal about what had happened to his friend. I had the human tell me exactly and precisely what happened, making sure that the grieving animal captured every image and every understanding. The grieving animal then told me again there had been no honoring, no ritual, no mention, nothing. I felt deeply moved by this animal's pain, and started to talk about honoring animals' spirits during and after transition.

At this moment something happened in that room that every human there still talks about when they are in contact with me. And when I remember it, even now as I type these words, tears of awe and Grace fill my eyes.

Every animal in the room quietly stood up and faced me. Even in that crowded room they managed to create a semi-circle around where I was standing, with their heads all pointing towards me. They all stayed in that position, almost motionless, completely silent, totally attentive, until I was complete in my description of the importance of honoring and ways of honoring the spirit. Even now, speaking on this topic in any gathering of animals and humans has instantly invited total attention from every animal present.

Gather all the care-humans and the animal friends you can in a room or area your animal loves or loved. Play music such as Gregorian chants, Baroque music or Mozart. Assemble all the physical items to play a part in your ritual. This could include photographs or rendered art. Collecting pictures and drawing one's beloved companion is particularly helpful for children.

Gather blue or golden-white blankets, to color-comfort both humans and animals alike. Light the white candle. Spend 30 to 45 minutes joyfully acknowledging or remembering your animal. When joy or at least attempts at joy, are associated with the animal's transition, the energies elevate much more quickly and the animal becomes beautifully clear even faster (in human terms).

If it comes to you to read poetry or from Wisdom literature or (for indoor animals) even to watch the favorite TV program you always watched together, as part of the honoring ritual, do so.

Send reassuring thoughts and images and speak soothing words to your animal. For reading from the Wisdom literature, the 23 Psalm from the Judao-Christian tradition is a powerful poem of transition and is quite appropriate. Ways of creatively using that beautiful Psalm are in the section in this book called, *The 23rd Psalm*. Another exquisite selection of Wisdom literature is from the Lamsa translation of the New Testament from the Christian tradition, specifically the Lord's Prayer spoken by the Master, Jesus Christ.

Many people create invitations with pictures of their animal friend and invite the care-humans to the ritual. Some create memorial brochures and distribute them to friends. Others create beautiful web-sites with pictures and quotations and email links to their friends. Some create delightful collages of various pictures from their life together with their animal companion and distribute them via mail or email. The choices are as endless as your imagination.

Creating a memorial for your animal friend may be especially healing for you. When a beloved dies, a part of us dies, too. Feeling your pain, grieving, accepting it, and moving forward, is helped by the cathartic work of creating a memorial.

I have noticed over the past several years the extraordinary healing that happens when care-humans create memorials, especially web-sites including poems and pictures and quotations and collages, and email the links to their friends. It is a beautiful form of memorialization, creating a legacy and sharing that is much appreciated by all in today's world. It is profoundly healing.

If you'd like to create a web memorial while also helping an animal charity, check with your local organizations, first, to support your community. If you aren't finding one that suits, Best Friends Animal Sanctuary is a good choice, they have a web-site with a place to post memorials. They are the largest sanctuary for abused and abandoned cats, dogs, and other animals in the United States. Email editor@bestfriends.org. The mission of Best Friends is "to help bring about a time when there are no more homeless pets, and when every cat or dog who's ever born can be guaranteed a good home with a loving family." You can also post a memorial at www.petloss.com.

If it comes to you to create your own poetry to express your feelings or even to help another in their grief and loss and to re-affirm your love for the grieving one who has lost an animal companion, do so. Such expressions are deeply appreciated, in my experience and observation.

My brother's daughter, my delightful and petite niece Jeneve, had three parakeets named after spices. Pepper and Ginger were the first pair, who passed away, then Parsley came along and lived longer, dying shortly after Jeneve left for college. Jeneve mourned their loss. My brother wrote this poem as comfort for Jeneve, nicknamed "NeeNee," to memorialize her love for her birds and to reaffirm his love for her.

Special Little One
(to NeeNee)

Pepper Ginger Parsley
three gentle spices
chirping
brightening each day
with their presence
on their perches
bringing us always to a place of singing
impossible to hold for us
but
so important a place to try to at least go.

Bird in a cage
which of us is caught
the one making each day
lighter

brighter
having long since lost the sense of containment
or
the other always worrying about the bars
in out
out in.

I would look forward to Parsley's proud
pronouncement of the sun of day from the perch
and
in pausing to listen
would in my heart and soul
not only feel a comforting place of position
peace
presence
but also a sound of aliveness
of laughter and connection to years
of living in a room
shared
with another little one so special
also gentle and perky and a delight
with a largeness of heart and soul
I also hear
chirping at the each of day
and
brightening the way for those that pause to listen.

About Oliver: *Oliver taught me that the reason animal communicators don't receive as many calls regarding birds is because birds are so much better at communicating with their humans (in the opinion of the birds!).*

Your Animal Friend, Your Veterinarian, and You

Alex

The more resonance and understanding you have of the process of assisting your animal friend's essence energy in separating from its physical form, the easier it will be on both of you. I offer the following to help promote such resonance.

Small animal veterinarians will participate sometimes in rituals or honorings performed at your home on behalf of your animal friends. Most, however, prefer to follow the procedures customary to their practice, which will depend on the species of animal. Of course, most large animal veterinarians go to the farm or stable to perform euthanasia; or trainers and/or care-humans perform this act. Small animal veterinarians preferring in-clinic procedures, point out that most animals empty their bladders and bowels due to the complete relaxation of all muscles, and the clinic is better equipped to handle this; plus, most animals are less defensive in an animal hospital situation than at home. They further point out that the clinic environment is better equipped to handle the proper care of the body.

You may feel you don't know how to act or what to do, what to expect of yourself, regarding contacting your veterinarian to ask for euthanasia assistance. This is normal.

If this is your first time, tell the receptionist. S/he will know your veterinarian's normal practice. If it's a small animal and you're going to the clinic, s/he will know when to make such an appointment so that your veterinarian is not feeling rushed with other appointments or surgery. Early morning appointments or the last appointment of the day is what many do.

Ask the receptionist what to expect. S/he will ask you what you'd like done with your animal friend's body. You can either take your deceased animal friend home for burial, or ask for cremation or burial through your veterinarian. Some animal clinics have animal cemeteries on their property; many know of ones in your area.

Your veterinarian may ask you if you'd like an autopsy performed. This is usually for a specific reason. Be at peace with the knowing that most veterinarians do not sell or otherwise experiment on deceased animals. Your animal's body will be well-treated.

When you arrive, check with the receptionist to see if you will have to wait. You may prefer to wait in your car, rather than waiting in the waiting room or an exam room. Your veterinarian may wish to have you administer a sedative at home before bringing your animal to the hospital.

When it's time, you have options. You can be there with your animal friend. You can wait in the waiting room, then briefly view your friend after the passing, or spend some moments in private with your friend.

This is a completely personal decision. I suggest to you, however, that I have never spoken to a care-human who didn't tell me s/he felt bad about being absent from their animal friend at the time of its passing. Most speak of feelings of abandoning their animal friend at this crucial time. This creates a sense of guilt that can live on for years.

Those who have been with their animal friends, however apprehensive they were at first, usually are deeply moved at the peace, the ease, and the silent speed of the process; and the extraordinary compassion of their veterinarians at this important time.

Very few humans are comfortable with death, including and especially your veterinarians and their technicians, even though they see it almost daily. I teach Reiki, a gentle energy healing modality. Many veterinarians and veterinary health technicians attend my classes, since many of my classes are oriented towards energy healing for animals.   Any discussion of euthanasia and preparing an animal energetically for euthanasia, brings the room to hysterical crying in a few seconds.   Know that your veterinarians and veterinary health technicians are deeply moved by the experience, regardless of how many times they live through it.   Consider them, also, in your decision.   Weigh your discomfort and apprehension in the moment, against the honoring, giving proper respect, and completion for your animal friend and all who loved and cared for it.

Take a human friend with you and let your human friend drive you home.   You will most likely be upset or crying and may not be able to see clearly.   Remember, very few humans, and this includes your veterinarian and his/her staff, get used to death.

For an animal to receive a humane death it needs to be rendered unconscious as rapidly as possible.   Most recommended methods of euthanasia therefore involve agents that affect the brain very rapidly. The actual process itself usually involves a sedative followed by a solution of chemicals administered intravenously and intended to effect a quick and painless termination of nerve transmission and subsequent muscle relaxation. The administering must be done within the vein for the procedure to unfold correctly.   Your animal may need to be restrained for this to occur.   You can offer to assist by holding your animal.

When the vein is found the veterinarian will inject the solution. In a matter of seconds your animal friend may take a deep breath then grow limp and appear to be in a deep sleep. Your friend is unconscious now.

If your animal's essence energy has already started to separate, which it will have if it is in 3rd stage, your animal may continue to breathe for a longer time than you may expect. This happens because your animal already has experienced "living" with its essence energy partially separated from form and in a state of semi-separation. It will simply take a little longer for the messages to get back and forth. When the sending and receiving is complete, the essence energy will separate entirely and your animal's breathing will cease.

After your animal friend's physical body has died it may need its eyelids closed. Do so gently and with the utmost respect and love. Sometimes looking into your animal friend's eyes after the separation of the essence energy from form is a sadness too deep to bear. We are so accustomed to seeing the essence energy which reflects through the eyes, that when we look at our animal friends' eyes after its passing and when the essence energy has left, it can be a very difficult experience. At this time, the essence energy is most likely hovering around you, but to many humans, it is no longer visible. Your veterinarian may do this gentle act of closing the eyes for you.

Most veterinarians at this time offer great support and empathy. If you're taking your animal friend's body home with you for burial, many will carry your friend's body out to your vehicle for you.

Bring the Euthanasia Prayer at the end of this little book with you. It will help you, your animal, your veterinarian, and his/her staff.

I have noticed that taking the Bach Flower Essence, Rescue Remedy, along with the Essence, Walnut, has been extremely helpful to both animals and humans at this time. Chicory, for the care-human, assists with letting go. Put four drops of Rescue Remedy, two drops of Walnut, and 2 drops of Chicory in a sterilized 30 ml tincture bottle. Fill the bottle to the shoulder with spring water or other pure water. Then take 4 drops of this mixture diluted in a small glass of pure water, as often as you need it. You also may put this same mixture into the water of any other animal companions in your household who will be affected by your animal friend's transition.

If it's too much for you to be with your animal at the actual time of euthanasia, know that your animal already knows this about you. Each person's spiritual ecology is different and your animal already knows yours. To our animals we are all completely transparent. Do what you can do. I offer again, that I have yet to talk to a human who didn't feel bad that they weren't with their animal friend at the time of its passing. I have also yet to talk to a human who was with an animal friend at the time of its passing, who did not experience peace, wonder, mystery, and spiritual elevation. This elevation is a form of palpable Grace. It lasts for weeks and will assist you mightily in your grieving. Having said this, please also know that some animals (and humans, too) orchestrate the timing of their deaths intentionally so that their beloved care-humans are not present.

About Alex: Alex is a Sheltie adopted from a kill-shelter in June, 2001. Alex is one of the gentlest souls I've ever met. Alex quickly taught me that all I have to do when I want something is to simply ask from a place of good-natured, gentle, loving non-attachment. I used to believe that I had to be prepared for not getting what I asked for or to be prepared for having to fight or push for it.

Fyodor Dostoyevsky

Love the animals, love the plants, love every thing. If you love everything, you will perceive the divine mystery in things. Once you perceive it, you will begin to comprehend it better every day. And you will come to love the whole world with an all-embracing love.

About The Grief

Tigger & Tabatha

The grief you may feel at the passing of your animal friend is very real. I have observed that grief is often a more lasting and binding experience for those who are still in human form than love. Our planet learned this in August 1997 with the closely timed passing of Princess Diana and Mother Teresa, when much of our globe was joined in profound grief. More recently, we experienced it again, in September 2001, when terrorist-instigated attacks in the United States resulted in great loss of life.

The positive aspect of grief is its catalytic action towards emotional and spiritual growth. Grief plants focus on the loved ones and their loss like a seed, to ultimately express through those of us who have experienced bereavement, as compassion, beauty, service and love for those whose lives touch ours and whose lives we touch.

The other side of grief is its potential for becoming a catalyst for helplessness, sadness, and clinical depression. There are many support groups available to those who express grief in this way, including wonderful web communities.

When we are mindful, sensations of grief, anger, loss, or guilt temporarily evaporate, so we can help our companion's passage out of body as easily and comfortably as possible. Yet when our animal friend's death is complete, we often feel desperately alone.

You will probably experience the sense of the living energetic essence of your animal friend around you in your home and/or in your yard or on your grounds after the physical body is gone. This is normal for one who is connected by love to an animal friend. Your animal's essence energy is indeed present. There is a heightened spiritual awareness that comes after profound loss. Your sense perception is sufficiently elevated to be able to receive the sensations. If you have anything else you'd like to say to your animal friend, do so. If you are particularly quiet inside you may also hear your friend's replies. Although it takes great energy for them to do so, animals who have crossed over can move physical belongings around as an indicator of their continued presence in and awareness of their human companion's life.

Rune's human, Barbara, left his food and water dish out for several weeks after he crossed over. Whenever she was away he would move the dish.

Most of the animals I've sensed after separating from form have had only love and gratitude for their care-humans. They are usually quite specific about the items and incidents that were special to them and often offer great detail about them. They care deeply for the well-being of those they loved in form. They feel deep compassion at the sight of their loved ones in pain. They want their care-humans to know that they are okay.

The grief you feel is no insult to those who love you and are still in form or those whom you love. It comes from a deep aching for what once was, from a deep sadness that sometimes seems too deep to bear, until you remember that the living essence energy of your friend has separated from its physical form and is on its way.

I've learned from helping so many through the grief process that grief is not the only strong emotion humans feel at this time. Many humans tend to add self-criticism to the grief of loss. Frequently, such sentences start with, *"If only..."* or *"I wish I..."* Some feel anger. Some want to find someone to blame. Memories arise of other losses or abandonments. Often, we chasten ourselves for being so upset. We cringe inside at people who say, *"It's only a ..."* Or, *"You can always get another one."* We want to explode in anger and tell them they don't understand how special this animal friend, this relationship has been to us and that we will always remember.

Our animal friends are a source of love, knowingly and eternally connected to the unconditional Oneness, the giving and receiving of Divine love. When an animal friend's body dies, the experience in the present in physical form of that Love in an obvious way is removed. The loss of an animal friend is often a re-enactment of the separation from the Divine all over again. It is in this capacity that one of the deepest experiences of the human soul is activated. The deep experience I'm referring to is the loss of the eternal awareness of the infinite Grace of being surrounded by Divine Presence that happens to varying degrees when we are "born," when our living essence energy joins with a physical form that embraces life.

Animals are aware of death. They grieve and experience loss, too. Animals in your family who are still in form, will see the upset in you and your family, the crying. They may not know where the other animal friend (or human, in the event of a human passing) has gone. All they will want to do is find their beloved and missed animal or human companion. Many will wander and pace in the areas of the house or yard that the human or animal friend frequented. Many will wait for the human or animal friend to return. Some will patiently and loyally wait by doors, chairs, windows, fences, vehicles, shared spots under trees. Some stop eating. Some quite literally die of grief. The emptiness that follows a death never quite disappears.

It's not clear to me that we ever fully recover, because we are all touched and changed by each life. It's possible recovery may not even be an option. We do, however, adjust. And we can move into the energy of being joyous in the cycle of life. The choice of how to respond is ours alone.

You can help your animal friends still in form at this time. Tell your animal friends where their beloved animal or human friend has gone. Say that the living essence energy has separated from the physical body. Tell your animal friends whatever you know, about the cause and manner of the separation. Tell them where the physical body is and what is or will become of it (burial, cremation with ashes into an urn, cremation with ashes to be scattered, unknown, etc.). Speak with them in as clear and direct a manner as possible. Offer them clear, precise mental images. Your animal friend may appear to yawn, move away, groom him/her self, take a nap or watch you. No matter. Your friend is listening intently and understands.

If your grieving animal friend was not part of any ceremony or ritual, which is commonly the case with our animal friends when a beloved human has passed, create and perform one with your animals, for the loved one (animal or human), who has crossed over. Be sure to share exactly and precisely how you feel.

About Tigger and Tabatha: At a point in time when Tabatha was experiencing dangerous liver values, surgery was scheduled. Tigger knew ahead of time that Tabatha was going to have a difficult time coming out of the anaesthesia. He also knew that something would happen that would change their relationship forever, although he wasn't sure what. The night before the scheduled surgery, Tigger was sitting in his Simba chair while Tabatha was walking around. Tabatha went to go to sit in the chair, but couldn't because of limited space. Tigger suddenly reached out and grabbed her and pulled her as close to him as he could, hugging her and sharing intimacy and prescient grief for quite some time. Their care-human Karen was struck by the extremely uncharacteristic behavior and had more than enough time to take this picture.

Tigger was quite correct. His and Tabatha's relationship changed dramatically. The former closeness and intimacy ended when post-surgery Tabatha came home emitting an odor extremely disturbing and repulsive to Tigger.

Nicole and Neasa

Parent to Child

*I*n the attempt to explain death adults frequently confuse, frighten or distance children. The best course of action is to feel what you are feeling; identify it; express it as clearly as you can; and tell the Truth.

As you are an open book emotionally and telepathically to your animals, so too are you to your children, especially those seven years of age and under. Whatever you feel and think passes energetically to them. If you are uncomfortable talking about death, glamorize or romanticize it, create an association that can elicit fear in the child's mind or abort all questions and feelings, whatever your experience, the energetic packet of such messages is conveyed to your child.

Children are sponges, absorbing, observing, growing, responding to their environments, simultaneously learning beliefs, attitudes, and behaviors. Most take their cues from what's happening around them.

My extensive experience includes counseling people even 50 years after the death of a loved one. I have come to believe the best approach is Truth. Truth will always be the specific movement or lack of movement in the moment. Such Truth will always transcend culture, country, belief system, or language. An example: "Rudy's body has died. This means his body can't feel any more and isn't breathing or eating. His body isn't going to be with us any more. His body will go back to the earth, like a leaf does, that has died and fallen from the tree to the ground.

"His spirit, that part of him which we all felt when we thought of

him or played with him or loved him or took care of him, will stay alive, especially in our hearts and in our memories."

It is absolutely best, I have found, to have a ritual like the ones suggested in this book. Encourage the children to say something or show something about their animal friend. Do your best to encourage some joyful appreciation of the animal companion whose body has died.

Exactly how a specific child will react will vary from moment to moment and with the emotional age of the child. Children who are still in touch with spirit, usually those under seven years of age, know at some level that death isn't final and is a death of the physical body only. They evidence this by thinking that the one who has died will be present at some future event.

Child: *"Snowy will be at my birthday party."*

Recommended Response: *"Snowy's spirit may be at your birthday party."*

Message: Affirmation of the child's intuitive knowing.

Children at almost any age (and sometimes adults!) can have a fear of having influenced or caused the death and therefore can experience guilt. Perhaps at one point they secretly wished their animal friend dead and now it is. Whether your child expresses this to you or not will depend on the child. Be as specific as you can about the exact cause of the physical death of the animal's body.

Recommended Response: *"Rudy's body died because his lungs stopped working. When the lungs stop working our bodies can't breathe, and when our bodies can't breathe, they can't live."*

Message: Gives a reason outside of the child's influence for the animal's physical death.

Children a little older, six to eight years, are still influenced by their deep soul's knowing that essence energies live on after the death of the physical body. They may reminisce about the animal that has passed, look at pictures, or evidence playing with their friend. Children are still somewhat open to the energy at this point and are usually responding to the efforts of the essence energy that has crossed over, to be in touch with them and let them know they are okay. This behavior can last for months or even up to a year. Usually, when it stops, the essence energy has moved on.

Recommended Response: Allow the children their remembrances.

Message: Affirmation of their memories of love.

Other reactions can include:

"Can I still play with {human friend's name} ..." Children under five want to know the impact on their immediate, anticipated plans. Often they will ask the seemingly unrelated, *"Can I still play with Jonathan?"*

Recommended Response: Answer them with whatever's so.

"What will change..." Children from seven to eleven often want to know what will change and what will stay the same.

Recommended Response: Answer as best you can, including, *"I don't know yet."*

"It's no big deal..." Pre-teen or teen-age children sometimes evidence flippancy, cavalier attitudes, or detachment. These are commonly called "defense mechanisms" and come from the fear of losing emotional control or being opened up to criticism, especially from peers.

Recommended Response: *"If you'd like to talk to me privately about Rudy, let me know. Or you can write out how you're feeling."*

There are a few trouble-maker sentences, I have found, in my years of experience as a counselor:

"Don't feel bad, Rudy's in doggie heaven."

This can have loaded messages. If you are feeling sad inside, crying inside or out, this sentence gives the message that feeling sad isn't okay and perhaps also the larger message that showing strong feelings isn't appropriate. Additional mixed messages are that Rudy is now away and somewhere else, exactly as he once was here, but the child can't see him anymore and hence contains the hidden message that Rudy has been "taken" away. Children are used to having things taken away from them when they've been bad, so the hidden message here can be that the child was somehow bad or did something wrong, and that's why Rudy was taken away and is gone.

"God has taken Rudy because Rudy was so loving and good." This sentence is tied with the next one for being the most terrifying and confusing for children and one the energy of which seems to haunt some adults many decades later. The child now wonders, should I be good, or should I be bad? If very good, the child reasons, s/he will be taken out of the existing circumstances; if very bad, s/he gets to stay around. There is also the embedded messages that God only takes what's good, so inherently, what isn't with God, is bad; and the child therefore can start to see him/herself as bad. An even bigger issue raised in the child's mind, is how could a God of love take away a beloved animal friend and cause everyone to cry?

"Rudy's gone to sleep and he's not going to wake up." This one is tied with the previous one for causing the most problems decades later. The child now fears sleep, either going to sleep itself, because the child may not wake up either; or fears that the parents, when they go to sleep, may die, too. A better response is to speak in terms of the death of the physical body of your animal companion while assuring your child that you intend to be here in your child's life until way after the child is grown up.

About Nicole and Neasa: Nicole, of course, is my daughter, pictured here when she was 8 years old with our Golden Retriever, Neasa. Neasa was named for the Princess of the Ewoks in Return of the Jedi. Neasa played a magnificent part in our lives, providing stability and love for Nicole while her father and I were divorcing. In the Spring of 2001, while a speaker at the Comfort Caring Canines Annual Meeting in Pennsylvania, I met Neasa again: this time as Belle, named by her current care-humans, again a Golden Retriever and again providing stability and love for a young girl whose parents are divorcing.

Part III:

Prayers, Rituals, and Healing Words

Black Elk

We should understand well that all things are the work of the Great
Spirit. We should know the Great Spirit is within all things: the
trees, the grasses, the rivers, the mountains, and the four-legged and
winged peoples; and even more important, we should understand
that the Great Spirit is also above all these things and peoples. When
we do understand all this deeply in our hearts, then we will fear, and
love, and know the Great Spirit, and then we will be and act and live
as the Spirit intends.

Every day, in every way,
I'm doing better and better...

Tabatha

About Healing Sounds, Words and Prayers

$\mathscr{I}$m going to share now a very brief summary of what I've learned over five decades of extensive travel and study about language, sounding, chants, prayers and healing words.

The nature of the earth as vibration and the healing power of sound are well documented in many sources. Suffice to summarize that what we say and think and particularly the emotionally-charged sounds we utter are extremely powerful and have major healing properties; that certain sounds are more powerful and clearer than others; and that therefore certain languages have far more powerful co-creative manifest energy than others. The higher the level of vibration, the higher the Inspiration, the closer to Source, the more powerful the healing which manifests. This energy is what I believe is within the world's Wisdom Literature. It is a Truth that immersing one's self in the energetic of Wisdom Words heals.

One aspect all sounds have in common: when sounds of clear vibration are emitted from the centered power of a congruent and passionate heart, they ALWAYS influence the Universe. Whether we call such sounds prayers, healing words, affirmations, exclamations, exultation, decrees, chants, or soundings makes no difference. When the feelings of our hearts align with the thoughts in our minds and the intensity of our wills and we put that into the congruent action of using our bodies in creating thought, making clear vibration and/or uttering sound, we have a result that gets the attention of the Universe.

Don Campbell teaches us the healing importance, as humans, of a "daily vowel movement," taking the range of vowel sounds through the range of the individual's voice daily. Qi Gong practice has used sound to heal the internal organs for millennia. Most traditions including both religious and shamanic traditions, use sound to in-fill, inspire, connect, heal and calm.

Sound is used constantly among our animal friends for expression and healing as well. Joyful chirps of morning welcome, contented purrs, delighted whinnies and nuzzles, happy barks, gregarious banters, dolphin whistles, all are sounds of expression. Sounds of nurturing and compassion exist in almost all species.

Sounds of nurturing and compassion heal. A great example occurs in the cat family. Elderly cats or cats who are infirm often vocalize to use sound to vibrate their bodies into healing frequencies. Cats are particularly energy aware and are particularly good at healing themselves. Although this practice of elderly cats can be irritating for their care-humans, I have been told (by the cats, of course!) that a wonderful way to both help your cat and minimize the amount of vocalizing, is to mimic it as best you can. If your cat is doing up and down octaves, then YOU do up and down octaves. If only up octaves, then you do up octaves. If only down, then you do down. Whatever sounds your elderly or infirm cat is making, are the sounds it intuitively knows will help it heal and/or help it live longer.

Be aware that when you mimic your cats, you'll be likely to draw some comments on your technique. Cats are pretty sure they're better at it than we are.

My advice to you for all the following prayers and healing words is to be aware not only of the meaning and the emotion of the words you are using but also the feeling of the words in your body as you conceive, form and utter them. In that way you will profoundly increase your congruency and therefore the power of the words you speak. An easy way to be sure you're feeling them is to put your hands on your heart and belly.

Prayer for me, is love radiated. It is the congruent inter-blending of the physical and the ethereal. When it is congruent, I dissolve myself into Divine clarity, softness and luminosity. Prayerful thought and word projected outward are powerful tools. If the word "prayer" bothers you, use the word "affirmation." When you pray (or affirm), neither elaborate or lengthy ritual nor a formal place of worship are necessary. A few seconds of completely congruent intention is worth hours of variably congruent and/or distracted ritual. Improvisation expressing from a core of love is better than recitation based in distraction, fear, or chaos.

Prayer for me, is focused, realized, compassionate intention, a process to bring myself into profound congruency and resonance on a condition or result; a process of setting myself in a place of expansion to be guided or led, especially on the subject matter of the prayer. Prayer is not pleading or supplication, begging, or taking power or authority away from myself; rather, it is aligning myself consciously with the power and authority of the Truth and the Universe of Divine Will, becoming that Truth, and helping it be made manifest.

Unless otherwise indicated, all the prayers in this section were inspired by specific situations and authored through me.

About Tabatha: Tabatha Alexis Cornell is a beautiful, blue-eyed flame-point Siamese born with a rare liver condition called extra-hepatic shunts. Tabatha's condition was deemed inoperable and incurable. She was given a short life expectancy. A major veterinary hospital recommended euthanasia.

Tabatha, however, had other ideas. She is now 5 years old and happily riding in convertibles and chasing chipmunks. She attributes her well being to finding me (Elizabeth) as her voice and Drs. Deva Khalsa and Robin Love to help her human on-goingly make the right decisions in her care.

Meister Eckhart

Apprehend God in all things,
for God is in all things.
Every single creature is full of God
and is a book about God.
Every creature is a word of God.

A Simple & Profoundly Powerful Prayer

(The following prayer is extremely powerful and suitable in almost all healing situations. I wrote it and use it extensively. Use the appropriate name and pronoun for your animal friend's situation).

May the White Light of Healing surround (animal friend's name) _____ and hold Its Resonance of Healing for and around her/him.

May all decisions on his/her well-being be wise.

May all care-takers be compassionate.

May Healing Grace be made manifest.

A Prayer of Decree for Specific Healing

(Payers of decree command in co-creative alignment with Divine Power and Authority. This is a powerful prayer I wrote and use when I know specifics of the situation).

Masters of Light, Angelic Forces, I am Presence and Higher Self, All Names of All that is Holy, we invite your healing and support now.

Enter into and in-fill the body of our beloved animal companion, {Name} _____. Heal this body, every cell. {Suggestion: Be specific with what you'd like healed. Examples: Hips, align. Joints, rejuvenate. Spinal column, align. Organs, heal. Body, balance. Cells, cleanse. Blood, fortify.}

Any disease that exists in this body, any deformity, anything that does not support vibrant health now, leave this body, never to return.

By All Names of all that is Holy, we declare this healing as Truth. By All Names of all that is Holy, we are thankful for this Grace.

And so it is.

Asking the Question

Archtika

*T*he process of death and the efforts of a care-human at the time of dying and death, transcend all religions and philosophies. Appropriate action will always come from the knowing and mercy deep within your heart. The following process may help you touch that knowing and mercy.

Go to your animal. Breathe deeply. When you make choices while breathing shallowly, you are using only your outer, rational mind, not your spirit or inner mind.

Center yourself as best you can. Clear your outer mind as best you can. Remember foremost your love for your animal and the highest good.

Turn your energy intently and lovingly to your animal and ask, "Are you ready to leave form now?"

Breathe deeply again.

Your animal will answer in that breath.

If you're not sure, repeat this procedure, and this time ask, "Will you please give me a sign, a behavior change, if and when you're ready, if and when you've entered the 3rd stage and are ready?"

The animals will always respond, "Yes," to this question. They will always give you a sign.

Then you pay attention.

If you're still not sure, repeat the procedure, and add, "Will you please make it very obvious, if you're in or when you've entered 3rd stage, and when you're ready?"

Your animal will show you a specific, easily recognizable sign; or you'll experience a profound knowing in your body. Some people report hearing a voice. Others have dreams in which other beloved animal or human companions who have crossed over, appear to them. Such dreams are messages usually of readiness and of preparation for welcoming.

About Archtika: Archtika is the new form of the essence energy formerly known as the wondrous and beautiful Kantischna. Kantischna/Archtika took her new form in late 2000. See the chapter entitled, "The Cycle of Life."

For Help in
Making the Decision

For the following prayer, please use whatever Name for the Divine works for you.

Divine Presence, make it so, that I know the course of action to take. Show me in such a direct and obvious way, that I can be at peace, knowing I won't overlook or fail to see the signs.

Make it so, that my animal friend, _____, knows absolutely my love.

Make it so, that my intention for service and right choices, be heard clearly.

Make it so, that my doubt is quieted and that what comes to me is correct action.

Make it so, that I appropriately honor the spirit and preferences of my beloved animal friend, _____, thereby realizing for all, peace and confirmation in the spiritual dimension.

Make it so, that I hold Mercy as my highest intent, meaning not necessarily doing what is convenient, economical, or practical at the moment, but rather what is correct on a very high level of consideration for another living being, while also considering being merciful, soft, and gentle with myself.

And it is so.

Memorial for an Animal Friend

Please use whatever Name for the Divine works for you.

Dear God, Creator of all creatures great and small, our beloved animal friend has left us and we gather today with sadness in our hearts. Ease our grief as we bid farewell to (animal friend's name) _____, whose passing has left a gap in our family circle.

S/he demanded so little of us: fresh water, food, sunlight, our companionship and our presence; and gave so much in return: uncritical, unlimited affection and devotion for all of us. Greeting each day, each moment, happily on his/her own terms, s/he showed us how to live in the present moment rather than regret the past or worry about the future.

Today we remember the playful moments, the quiet moments, and the love we shared. These are the memories of our animal friend that we will always cherish:

(List the things you remember most, for example: always understood how we were feeling, always showed us unconditional love, loved his/her sounds, personality traits, etc.)

Creator, we are grateful for being allowed to share her/his life for its allotted time. We will miss her/him in our family life, but s/he will always be present in our hearts.

Creator, we thank you for the days we spent with _____, for animal friends everywhere, and for all the wonderful creatures that you have placed upon our earth.

Brutus' Prayer

(The intent of this prayer is to help ease the transition and path of the essence energy after it's left form. I call this Brutus' prayer because I first wrote it for Brutus, a magnificent spirit in a canine body who transitioned on October 6, 2001. Please feel free to use whatever Name for the Divine works best for you. Use whatever name, date and pronouns are appropriate to your animal friend and situation).

Creator, we know the soul-spirit of our beloved (animal friend's name) _____ left its form on (date) _____. We know that after we've left form, it is our physical body only that dies; and that our consciousness continues, the awareness of our soul-spirit, our essence energy, continues.

We also know that the time of transition involves inquiries and reviews, and takes time known by humans sometimes, as weeks and even months or years.

We ask that this time for _____ be gentle and short and filled with Light, so that s/he may move peacefully and swiftly on to whatever his/her next choices are.

We send you light and love to help you on your journey.

We ask for all care-humans, the peace of this knowing.

And it is so.

The 23rd Psalm

The Lord is my Shepherd, I shall not want.
He maketh me to lie down in green pastures.
He leadeth me beside the still waters.
He restoreth my soul.
He leadeth me in the path of righteousness, for His name's sake.

Yea, though I walk through the valley of the shadow of death,
I will fear no evil; For Thou art with me.
Thy rod and thy staff, they comfort me.
Thou preparest a table before me, in the presence of my enemies.
My cup runneth over.
Surely, goodness and mercy shall follow me all the days of my
life,
And I shall dwell in the house of the Lord, forever.

KJV

The 23rd Psalm

The 23rd Psalm from the Judao-Christian tradition is powerfully viewed as a Psalm of provision, protection, guidance and healing during transition. Envision the Jewish people, wandering through a desert without provisions. The Psalm calls on the provision of daily sustenance (*I shall not want ... preparest a table*), the provision of nightly comforts (*green pastures*), the provision of nurturing protection *(thy rod and thy staff, they comfort...)*, the provision of healing *(restoreth my soul)* and the provision of the constant conscious presence of the Divine (*thou art with me*).

Think of your animal friend and the journey of its essence energy as it moves from an existence blended with living physical form to its shedding of any negativity and fear of its physical experience, to living again as pure essence energy. Speaking these words will help.

I recently completed my own translation from the Hebrew of this beautiful Psalm. The energy of it is such that if you like, you can change the words, as I often do when I help people through their animal's transitions. So instead of using "my" and "I", you can use your animal friend's name. Speak it from your heart.

I surround my vision of the animal friend in a cocoon of the brightest white light and present the cocoon to the Divine Presence in my heart-mind, as I say the sounds aloud. If the animal's essence energy has already separated from physical form, I image two cocoons, one containing the physical body and one containing the living energetic essence and present both. A recent example of one of my custom re-workings of this exquisite Psalm:

"Lord, you are Tara's Shepherd, Protector-Provider in all ways;
All that is needed for her, is provided.
Make it so, that she lie down at the end of her life, in green pastures;
Make it so, that she is beside waters quiet and still rather than raging.
Restore and heal her soul from any suffering, attachment or confusion.
Continue to lead her in the paths of correct and loving action, to resonate with the holy sound of your Sacred Name.
As she experiences this death and its illusion,
Let there be no fear of harm nor consequence of separation-thinking,
Since she is One with You. Your rod and staff comfort her.
You prepare all she needs for sustenance, in every moment, in the presence of any negative or harmful energies;
She has all that she could ever need.
Goodness and mercy follow her soul, through all the eternity;
She dwells in the Divine Oneness, forever."

Saying Goodbye

(Coming from the deepest part of the simplicity of your heart is best. This particular prayer, which I wrote, was inspired by an anonymous prayer I heard at a service once).

Today, I say Good-bye, God-speed.
I thank you for your love.
I thank you for choosing me.
I thank you for the joy I've experienced through you.
I thank you for the look in your eyes.
I thank you for the touch and feel of your body.
I thank you for the pleasure of watching you move.
I thank you for your sounds.
I thank you for your traits that I have so come to love.
I thank you for your loyalty.
I thank you for your compassion.
I thank you for your companionship.
I thank you for your endlessly generous spirit.
I thank you for sharing your life with me.
I thank you for trusting me.
I thank you for the lessons learned by virtue of our having been in each other's lives.
I thank you for the knowing, that even though I am now saying "Goodbye" and acknowledging my willingness to let you go, it is a paradox of life, that having let you go, you will nevertheless be with me always.
I love you. Go in peace.

Elizabeth Goudge

(1900-1984)

Nothing living should ever be treated with contempt. Whatever
it is that lives, a man, a tree, or a bird, should be touched gently,
because the time is short. Civilization is another word for
respect for life. . .

Euthanasia Prayer

(Dr. Bernie Spector and the staff of the Grey Fox Animal Hospital were the inspiration for this prayer, which I originally wrote for them. Euthanizing animals, especially those that have been intensely cared for, is one of the hardest things that veterinary professionals do. You are invited to share this prayer with your veterinarian and her/his staff. Please use whatever Name for the Divine works for you).

Divine Presence, we hold the life of your creature {Name} _____ in our hands. We affirm that when you gave humans dominion over all the earth this was not to include abusing, dominating, or treating in an arbitrary manner, the earth or the creatures in it; rather, it is to include care-taking, conscious use, enjoyment, nurturing of, learning from, and wise provision for the earth and all the creatures in it.

Today as we assist _____ in separating Spirit from Form, we remind ourselves of the original meaning of euthanasia: *eu*, or "good" and *thanatos*, or "death" . . . a dignified and painless method of dying, with the gentle intent to end suffering. We pray for a smooth transition for the Essence Energy of _____ and for understanding, forgiveness and blessings for all concerned.

We again affirm our personal intent to love, honor, nurture, and respect all living creatures.

And it is so.

Give Me Away

When I die, if you need to, weep.
Cry with your brother or sister
In whatever costume
Walking beside you
And when you need to put your arms around anyone
Give them what you need to give me.

I want to leave you something,
Something better than words or wounds.

Look for me in the humans and creatures we've known or loved
And if you cannot give me away
At least let me live in your eyes and heart
And not on your mind.

You can love me most
By letting hands touch
And bodies touch
And by letting go of those that need to be free.

Love doesn't die, bodies do,
So when all that's left of me is love,
Give me away.

Elizabeth

For Draining Grief

(When you're ready. Give yourself whatever time you need).

Close your eyes. Breathe deeply. Take yourself to the most beautiful place on earth you have ever seen or ever imagined . . .a mountaintop, the ocean, a deep forest. Breathe in and imagine yourself absorbing your exquisite surroundings, the different shades of the colors of the sky, the earth, the water or trees or lands around you. Begin to feel the comfort, the peace, the majesty around you.

Breathe deeply while you sit or stand quietly. Breathe in the smells and sounds around you. As you breathe out, open to the Divine Presence, allowing it to in-fill you. Repeat this. As you breathe in, breathe in your experience of Nature around you. As you breathe out, open to the Divine Presence, to in-fill you.

Breathe in your grief and pain. Let it circulate around you in your body. As you continue to inhale, consciously gift your pain and grief to the Divine Presence within and around you. In the moment of suspension between in-breath and out-breath, feel the Divine Presence transform your grief and pain.

Breathe out.

Breathe in a second time, consciously presenting your pain and grief to the Divine Presence, again allowing the Divine Presence to transform your grief and pain in this very moment. As you breathe out, begin to realize you can give something now, you are being rejuvenated, healed, through the Divine Presence.

Breathe in a third time. Consciously present all remaining pain and grief to the Divine Presence. Breathe out and feel all the pain and grief drain away. You can now present joy and peace to all creatures, all persons, everywhere.

Thornton Wilder

There is a land of the living and
a land of the dead
and the bridge is love
the only survival, the only meaning.

Communicating with an Essence Energy on The Other Side

(I am frequently asked if I feel it is possible to connect telepathically with the essence energy of an animal friend which is already crossed over. I do it all the time. This is what I do).

1. First, write out in advance, the specific questions you'd like answered.
2. Center yourself.
3. Light a candle, preferably white.
4. Pray and meditate for at least 20 minutes in whatever way works for you. Your goal here is to bring total emptiness and complete peace to your mind and complete connection through your heart.
5. When you feel you have reached a place of virtually no internal emotional movement or attachment to the reason for which you are meditating, look at (but don't think about) a picture or physical representation of the essence energy of the animal friend or creature companion who has crossed over and whom you'd like to contact.
6. Again without doing any thinking, look at the questions you've written down ahead of time; feel the questions in your heart; invite a response from the Divine; and write down whatever knowings come to you as you look with an infinitely expanded focus at the questions you've already written.
7. Thank the Divine profusely as well as the Essence Energy of the animal friend you've contacted.
8. Breathe deeply.
9. Extinguish your candle. You're done.

St. Francis of Assisi

Not to hurt our humble brethren (the animals) is our first duty to them, but to stop there is not enough. We have a higher mission: to be of service to them whenever they require it.

The Prayer of St. Francis of Assisi

(This is my favorite prayer).

Lord, make me an instrument of thy peace;

Where there is hatred, let me sow love;

Where there is injury, pardon;

Where there is discord, harmony;

Where there is doubt, faith;

Where there is despair, hope;

Where there is darkness, light;

Where there is sadness, joy.

Oh, Divine Master, grant that I may not, so much seek,

To be consoled, as to console;

To be understood, as to understand;

To be loved, as to love;

For it is in giving, that we receive;

It is, in pardoning, that we are pardoned;

It is in dying, that we are born to eternal life.

Plutarch

To the Dolphin alone, beyond all other, nature has granted what
the best philosophers seek: friendship for no advantage.

✷✷

About the Author

Elizabeth Forrest (Girard-diCarlo) Severino, D.D., D.R.S., Reiki Master, is a healing communicator for people and animals. She is currently living near the East Coast of the United States. She travels extensively as a practitioner and teacher of Spiritual Healing, Elements of Grace, Reverence for All Life, and Animal Communication.

Web-site: http://www.beyond1.com.

Email: Spirit1@beyond1.com.

Additional copies of this little book are available through the Internet, through your local bookstore, or by:

- Telephoning The Healing Connection at (856) 582-1700 (U.S.) or 01-856-582-1700 (International) or Fax (856) 582-0214 (U.S.) or 01-856-582-0214 (International). Price as of this printing (price is subject to change without notice): $29.95 U.S. per single copy for the Perfect Bound Edition; $49.95 U.S. for the Angel Edition (Collector's Edition). Add $6.50 U.S. for Shipping and Handling (U.S. S&H price only. Call or Fax for S&H pricing for other countries). Visa, MasterCard & Discover credit cards accepted.

- E-mailing Dr. Elizabeth Severino at spirit1@beyond1.com or ordering from the web-site: http://www.beyond1.com. Price as of this printing (price is subject to change without notice): $29.95 U.S. per single copy for the Perfect Bound Edition; $49.95 for the Angel Edition (Collector's). Add $6.50 U.S. for shipping and handling (U.S. S&H price only. Call for S&H pricing for other countries). Visa, MasterCard & Discover credit cards accepted.

- Mailing a check or money order payable to Dr. Elizabeth F. Severino or printed order form with credit card information to: The Healing Connection, P.O. Box 8469, Turnersville, NJ 08012-8469 U.S.A. Visa, MasterCard & Discover credit cards accepted.

Thank you for caring!